KATIE BROWN
CELEBRATES

KATIE BROWN
CELEBRATES

SIMPLE AND SPECTACULAR PARTIES ALL YEAR ROUND

PHOTOGRAPHY BY PAUL WHICHELOE

Little, Brown and Company

NEW YORK · BOSTON · LONDON

Little, Brown and Company
Hachette Book Group USA
237 Park Avenue, New York, NY 10017
Visit our Web site at www.HachetteBookGroupUSA.com

Little, Brown and Company is a division of Hachette Book Group USA, Inc.
The Little, Brown name and logo are trademarks of Hachette Book Group USA, Inc.

First Edition: November 2008

Library of Congress Cataloging-in-Publication Data
Brown, Katie.
    Katie Brown celebrates : simple and spectacular parties all year round / Katie
Brown.—1st ed.
        p.   cm.
ISBN-13: 978-0-316-11818-7
ISBN-10: 0-316-11818-4
1. Parties.   2. Cookery.   3. Menus.   4. Party decorations.   I. Title.
TX731.B758 2008
642'.4—dc22   2008005031

10   9   8   7   6   5   4   3   2   1

Printed in Singapore

Prentiss Crockett Corbin,
You give me reason to celebrate every day.

Contents

INTRODUCTION

i still remember the very first Christmas I spent away from home. The doorbell rang and the mailman handed me a letter. Immediately, I recognized my mother's handwriting and felt incredibly homesick. I tore open the letter, looking for any type of holiday comfort, as I was miles away from my family.

In hopes of easing my loneliness, my mother had put into words the joy and honor she felt having had—as she described it—the privilege of spending so many Christmases with me growing up. Although I was missed that year, she was sure there would be more festivities right around the corner, more occasions that I could infuse with my spirit of the season. As if she were slowly decorating a towering Christmas tree, she proceeded to share memories with the same care as hanging ornaments. She described the glee in my eye as I wrapped gifts for everyone in my family. She recounted the immense pride I took in playing the little drummer boy in our homemade pageant (you must understand that this was the first and only time my older sister let me play anything other than one of the farm animals). Then she reminded me of the excitement I displayed when we selected a donkey piñata for my eleventh-birthday party, and how I insisted on collecting special sticks that I then hand-painted for the event. I could hear her laugh through the letter as she described the time the fire department was called when I lit my kitchen on fire making batik sarongs for each of my guests in preparation for my first-ever sleepover. And, of course, the Christmas I arrived home from college and, having never prepared more than a box of mac and cheese, enthusiastically insisted on cooking the big buffet dinner for fifty celebrating my sister's graduation.

Not only was it a touching letter, it was also a ton of fun to read. And as I reminisce even now about parties past, I realize that the spirit she described in her letter has only gotten stronger. I've never had a hard time finding a good reason to celebrate, regardless of the occasion or circumstances. After all, the art of celebration is what makes life fun—it is what creates traditions and memories. I remind my team at the Katie Brown Workshop that we have the privilege of teaching people about the fun things in life . . . the icing on the cake, as we say. And to me there is nothing more fun than a party. Here you'll find that the party continues from my family holidays right onto the pages of this book. We had a party as we conceived it, prepared it, shot it, and wrote it.

My mom was onto something—I started preparing for this book during those childhood holidays, making this an obvious choice for my fifth and most important book. May this book inspire you to embrace an occasion. May this book encourage you to treat your next fete with love and care. The following pages are filled with simple and easy recipes, and tabletop ideas that are surefire ways to inspire you to celebrate and celebrate often, no matter what the occasion.

Tabletop

ALL THAT GLITTERS

DESSERT REFLECTION TRAY

PARTY BALLS

Menu

PARMESAN SOUP WITH
SWISS CHARD–STUFFED DUMPLINGS

FILET OF BEEF PILED HIGH WITH
MUSHROOMS AND FRIED LEEKS

GORGONZOLA-STUFFED POTATOES

ENDIVE SALAD WITH
WATERCRESS AND GRAPEFRUIT

EASY CHOCOLATE MOUSSE, THREE WAYS

CHOCOLATE CHUNKS WITH
CHERRIES AND PISTACHIOS

january
A NEW YEAR'S EVENING

january
A NEW YEAR'S EVENING

my most memorable New Year's Eve took place in my hometown of Petoskey, Michigan. I was eleven years old, and the big plans for the evening included watching the ball drop in Times Square on TV with my sisters and brother. My mother and father, not usually big partygoers, decided to make an exception and attend a fancy party. I remember being awestruck as they descended the stairs, my mother in a long black gown with silver trim and my father in a jet-black tuxedo. The image took my breath away. They were completely transformed. They said their good-byes as my sisters and I settled on the couch. My brother, though, had mysteriously disappeared. Moments before the final countdown, he reappeared carrying some type of contraption. It was a ball that hung over the door, with a long handle that he pulled when the clock struck midnight, his own six-year-old version of the Times Square ball drop. The mix of his enthusiasm and the warmth of seeing my mother and father shine so bright made the night seem just as exciting in Petoskey as it did in New York City. This celebration chapter combines my parents' glamour with my brother's excitement and ingenuity that New Year's Eve. Enjoy, and happy new year!

ALL THAT GLITTERS

This eye-catching centerpiece pays homage to the ball that drops in Times Square, and I believe the sparkling, silvery tinsel adds just the right touch of glamour.

Materials

10 FEET OF COPPER COIL

SILVER METALLIC SPRAY PAINT

SEVERAL STYROFOAM BALLS IN VARIOUS SIZES

SEVERAL FEET OF SILVER TINSEL GARLAND PER STYROFOAM BALL

GREENING PINS

Tools

PIPE CUTTER

SCISSORS

PEN

COIL STAND

· Cut the copper coil in half with a pipe cutter.

· Slightly uncoil each half of the pipe until it reaches around 2 feet tall, ensuring you have a sturdy circular base.

· Spray paint the copper coils silver and let them dry.

BALLS

· Wrap the tinsel garland around the Styrofoam balls until completely covered, securing with greening pins.

· Poke holes in the two largest balls with a pen and place them on top of the silver pipe stands. Place the remaining, smaller balls on the table to create a festive and sparkling centerpiece!

NOTE: THE AMOUNT OF GARLAND NEEDED TO COVER THE STYROFOAM BALLS DEPENDS ON THE THICKNESS OF THE GARLAND AND THE SIZE OF THE BALLS.

DESSERT REFLECTION TRAY

There's no better way to show off simple mousse than by placing bite-size portions on spoons and serving them on a mirrored tray, especially one you make yourself in a few easy steps. Make sure you prepare enough spoonfuls to fill all your guests with the chocolate delight (see recipe on page 25).

Materials

4 GLASS DRAWER KNOBS
   (THESE WILL SERVE AS LEGS FOR
   YOUR TRAY)

1 SQUARE MIRROR

Using glass glue, adhere one plastic knob to each corner of the back of the mirror.

Tools

GLASS GLUE

PARTY BALLS

These simple favors add fun and conversation to any gathering. It is useful to seal each ball with an initialed label to personalize these little treasures. You can also use them as place cards. We put candy in ours, but your favor balls can be tailored to any occasion—enclose little toys for a kids' party, fortunes for a birthday party . . . The sky's the limit!

Materials

FOUR FEET EACH OF WHITE, GRAY, AND BLACK CREPE PAPER

CANDY

DECORATIVE STICKERS (WITH INITIALS OF GUESTS IF DESIRED)

Tools

SCISSORS

RUBBER CEMENT

- Wrap a piece of candy in a strip of crepe paper as you begin to form a ball. Every few passes, add in another piece of candy.

- Glue a new strip of crepe paper (in a different color) to the end of the first. Continue wrapping in candy.

- Wrap until you have a palm-size ball. Then fasten the loose crepe paper tail with a decorative sticker.

PARMESAN SOUP WITH SWISS CHARD–STUFFED DUMPLINGS

Serves 6

This is an elegant way to start the new year. Just remember when using wonton wrappers to work in small batches and keep the wrappers covered with a damp paper towel to avoid them drying out.

Soup

1 TABLESPOON OLIVE OIL

1 CUP CHOPPED ONION

2 CUPS CHOPPED LEEK GREENS

2 CLOVES GARLIC, CRUSHED

4 SPRIGS FRESH THYME

6 PARSLEY STEMS

½ TEASPOON WHOLE BLACK PEPPERCORNS

3 (32-OUNCE) CONTAINERS LOW-SODIUM CHICKEN STOCK

2 PIECES PARMESAN RIND (ROUGHLY 5 X 2 INCHES EACH)

½ CUP FRESH PARSLEY LEAVES FOR GARNISH

Dumplings

2 TABLESPOONS OLIVE OIL

½ CUP CHOPPED ONION

2 CLOVES GARLIC, CHOPPED

6 CUPS WHITE SWISS CHARD (CLEANED OF STEMS), CHOPPED

1 CUP WATER

¼ CUP GRATED PARMESAN

SALT AND BLACK PEPPER TO TASTE

18 WONTON WRAPPERS (SQUARE)

1. For the soup: heat olive oil, onion, leeks, and garlic in a large stock- or soup pot on medium until onions and leeks are soft.

2. Stir in thyme, parsley stems, peppercorns, chicken stock, and Parmesan rind, and simmer for 40 minutes. Strain through a fine mesh strainer. Reserve the soup in a large soup or stockpot and discard solids.

3. For the dumplings: in a sauté pan, heat olive oil, onion, and garlic on medium until onions are translucent. Add Swiss chard and cook for eight minutes, stirring often. Add water, cover pan with a lid, and continue to cook until chard is tender. Remove pan from heat, drain any excess water, stir in Parmesan, and season with salt and pepper. Allow mixture to cool.

4. Place ½ tablespoon of mixture into the center of each wonton wrapper.

5. Dip your finger in water and slightly dampen the edges of a wonton wrapper, then join all 4 corners in the middle, making sure to seal any gaps. Repeat with other wrappers.

6. Bring soup to a boil and drop wontons into pot. Once they rise to the surface, continue to cook for 4 more minutes.

7. Fill each serving bowl with 3 wontons and cover with 1 cup of hot soup. Garnish with parsley.

FILET OF BEEF PILED HIGH WITH MUSHROOMS AND FRIED LEEKS

Serves 6

My father always said, "If you can cook a perfect steak, you've really made it as a cook!" Although I'm not sure I fully agree with him, I promise your guests will think you're a great cook after enjoying this tasty dish.

Leek Topping

5 CUPS VEGETABLE OIL

3 LEEKS

½ CUP FRESH PARSLEY LEAVES

¼ CUP FRESH ROSEMARY LEAVES, PICKED FROM STEM

¾ CUP ALL-PURPOSE FLOUR

SALT TO TASTE

Beef

½ CUP VEGETABLE OIL

6 (6-OUNCE) CUTS FILET MIGNON

SALT TO TASTE

COARSELY GROUND BLACK PEPPER TO TASTE

½ STICK BUTTER

4 CLOVES GARLIC, CRUSHED

3 SPRIGS FRESH THYME

3 SPRIGS FRESH ROSEMARY

Mushroom Topping

2 CUPS QUARTERED SHITAKE MUSHROOMS (STEMS REMOVED)

2 CUPS QUARTERED CRIMINI MUSHROOMS

2 CUPS QUARTERED OYSTER MUSHROOMS

2 TABLESPOONS SHERRY VINEGAR

5 TABLESPOONS UNSALTED BUTTER

SALT AND BLACK PEPPER TO TASTE

1. For the leek topping: fill a large pot halfway with oil, and heat on medium-high. (Test the temperature of the oil by sprinkling a small amount of flour into it; when the oil foams or sizzles, it is ready to fry.)

2. Cut white base from leeks and discard. Rinse the remainder and cut into small strips. Place strips in a large zip-locking plastic bag, add parsley, rosemary, and flour, and shake to coat evenly.

3. Remove leeks and herbs from bag, lower into oil, and fry until golden brown. Transfer with a slotted spoon onto a paper towel and season with salt.

4. For the beef: heat two large frying pans with ¼ cup of the vegetable oil in each on high. Season beef well on all sides with salt and pepper.

5. When pans are smoking hot, carefully place three filets in each pan, and lower heat to medium-high. Sear filets until golden brown on each side, about 4 minutes on each side for medium-rare. Add half of the butter, garlic, thyme, and rosemary to each pan during the last 2 minutes of cooking, spooning butter over steak as it cooks.

6. Remove filets to a plate to rest, and add mushrooms to hot pans. Cook for five minutes, browning on all sides. Add sherry vinegar and butter and cook until butter has melted. Season with salt and pepper to taste.

7. Mound warm mushrooms over each filet and pile high with fried leeks.

GORGONZOLA-STUFFED POTATOES

Serves 6

The Gorgonzola filling gives a bite to this ordinary baked spud. You'll stuff yourself with these delectable stuffed potatoes!

6   MEDIUM-SIZE YUKON GOLD
    POTATOES

2   TABLESPOONS VEGETABLE OIL

2   TABLESPOONS SALT

6   SQUARES ALUMINUM FOIL

⅓   CUP GORGONZOLA OR BLUE
    CHEESE

1   TEASPOON BLACK PEPPER

⅓   CUP HEAVY CREAM

¼   CUP CHOPPED CHIVES FOR
    GARNISH (OPTIONAL)

1. Preheat oven to 350 degrees.

2. Wash and dry potatoes, and place in a large mixing bowl. Toss with oil and salt. Wrap each potato individually with aluminum foil. Place potatoes on baking sheet, and bake until a toothpick is inserted with ease, approximately 45 minutes.

3. Remove potatoes from oven, remove foil, and allow potatoes to cool enough to handle. With a knife, cut one quarter-size hole in the top of each potato. With a small spoon, hollow out each potato. Reserve the potato flesh in a separate bowl.

4. Mash potato flesh and mix with the Gorgonzola, pepper, and cream. Stuff the potato shells with the mixture. Return potatoes to baking sheet and place under broiler until golden, about 5 minutes. Garnish with chives if desired.

ENDIVE SALAD WITH
WATERCRESS AND GRAPEFRUIT

Serves 6

The thing to remember about this zesty salad is to wait until just before serving to dress it. If you can't find watercress, use arugula.

2   BUNCHES WATERCRESS

2   RUBY RED GRAPEFRUITS, PEELED AND CUT INTO SEGMENTS

3   WHITE ENDIVES

¼   CUP CHOPPED CHIVES (OPTIONAL)

    JUICE OF 2 LEMONS

    JUICE OF 2 ORANGES

⅓   CUP OLIVE OIL

    SALT AND BLACK PEPPER TO TASTE

1. Wash watercress and dry.

2. Cut off root ends of endives, separate leaves, and place in a serving bowl. Add watercress and grapefruit, dress with lemon juice, orange juice, and olive oil, and season to taste with salt and pepper.

EASY CHOCOLATE MOUSSE, THREE WAYS

Serves 6 (makes approximately 18 spoonfuls)

With chocolate mousse this good and this easy,
you can give your guests a delicious start to the new year!

8 OUNCES SEMISWEET BAKER'S CHOCOLATE, CHOPPED

2 (8-OUNCE) CONTAINERS COOL WHIP TOPPING

1. Place chocolate in a large microwaveable bowl. Melt in microwave for 2 minutes, stirring every 30 seconds. Stir chocolate until smooth.

2. Once chocolate cools, add 1 cup of the Cool Whip to chocolate, stirring quickly. Continue folding in the rest of the Cool Whip in 2 batches, until there are no visible streaks.

3. Divide mousse into thirds.

Basic Chocolate Mousse

½ CUP TOASTED COCONUT, SLIVERED NUTS, OR CRUSHED CANDY

Place one-third of the mousse in a medium-size zip-locking plastic bag, cut off one corner, and pipe mousse onto 6 spoons, about 1 tablespoon per spoon. Top with your favorite topping, such as toasted coconut, slivered nuts, or crushed candy.

Malted Chocolate Mousse

⅓ CUP MALTED MILK POWDER

½ CUP WHOPPERS CANDIES, CRUSHED

Fold malted milk powder into one-third of the mousse. Place mixture in a medium-size zip-locking plastic bag. Pipe onto 6 spoons and top with crushed Whoppers.

Chocolate-Amaretto Mousse

3 TABLESPOONS AMARETTO LIQUEUR

½ CUP SLIVERED ALMONDS, TOASTED

Fold amaretto into one-third of the mousse. Place mixture in a medium-size zip-locking plastic bag. Pipe onto 6 spoons and top with toasted almond slivers.

CHOCOLATE CHUNKS WITH CHERRIES AND PISTACHIOS

Serves 6 (makes one 9 x 9-inch pan)

You thought chocolate was good? Try chocolate with cherries and pistachios. Heaven!

12 OUNCES BITTERSWEET BAKER'S CHOCOLATE, CHOPPED

½ CUP WHOLE MILK

3 TABLESPOONS UNSALTED BUTTER

¼ TEASPOON SALT

1 CUP SHELLED PISTACHIOS

1 CUP DRIED TART CHERRIES

1. In a large microwaveable bowl, combine chocolate, milk, butter, and salt. Place bowl in microwave and heat on high for 3 minutes, stirring every 30 seconds. Remove and whisk until combined and smooth. (If chocolate is not completely melted after whisking, return to microwave for 1 minute and repeat step.)

2. Stir in pistachios and cherries. Line the bottom and sides of a 9 x 9-inch pan with plastic wrap. Pour chocolate mixture into pan, scraping bowl, and smooth out evenly. Refrigerate until firm, about 1 hour.

3. Remove pan from refrigerator and invert chocolate mixture onto a cutting board. Remove plastic and cut chocolate with a knife into desired shape and size. Serve at room temperature.

february
A BIRTHDAY VALENTINE

i have a sister and her name is Marlee, Marion Leigh to be exact. All my life I have considered her as near to perfect as any human could possibly be. She is breathtakingly beautiful—you know the kind, whose wavy hair always looks just right with little to no effort, a big friendly smile, and the rosiest cheeks you ever saw. At the risk of sounding clichéd, my sister is as beautiful on the inside as she is on the outside. She was always a friend to the boy that everyone made fun of, she takes the blame if anyone is in trouble so the uncomfortable disagreement ends quickly, and she has never complained about anything that I can remember. In my early years of struggling to invent a life for myself in New York, she was the one I would call to tell of my latest plan to make ends meet, to which she would always respond with positive reinforcement. When I was opening in some off-off-off-Broadway show in New York or LA, there was Marlee all the way from Michigan in the front row. Breakup after breakup, it was either off to her home to recover or she to mine until I could get back on my feet, and believe me this was not an unusual occurrence, seeing as I waited till I was forty to wed. (Let's just say I kissed a lot of frogs.) To illustrate the depth of her perfection, the universe brought Marlee into this world on Valentine's Day. Literally a sweet heart born on sweetheart day.

You see, I believe Valentine's Day is not just for lovers but a day to honor all those we love. That is why Marlee's February 14 birthday makes so much sense. It was that day every year that I could remind her of the love I feel toward her as well as celebrate the romantic love in my life. So don't be afraid to wander a bit from Lovers' Lane this month and pay tribute to the other loves in your life. Whether it's a traditional Valentine celebration or a party to honor a longtime friend or family member, be sure to center your gathering around love. And there is no better way to do it than by taking the chill out of the February air with a hearty and hot bowl of stew followed by the ever-sexy finger food for dessert.

ROCKY RINGS

Predrilled slate circles that you can purchase at www.kulpscrafts.com can easily be turned into stylish napkin rings.

Materials

WIRE

5-INCH SLATE CIRCLES
WITH 2 PREDRILLED HOLES

Tools

WIRE CUTTER

· Cut the wire into 6-inch lengths.

· Weave the wires through the holes in the slate circles and twist the ends together.

· Roll the napkins and place them inside your rugged rings!

NOT-SO-EMPTY NEST

I think it is so special to gather bits of nature and create a miniature world that can be viewed through glass. It makes us take notice of the beauty around us, not to mention giving a certain depth to any tabletop.

Materials

GRAPEVINE

FLORAL FOAM

SPANISH MOSS

ROCKS

FLOWERS

GLASS CLOCHE

· Wrap the grapevine into a ring about 6 inches in diameter.

· Place the floral foam in the center of the ring and cover it with moss.

· Arrange the flowers in the foam by poking through the moss and into the foam.

· Arrange rocks around the flowers and cover with the glass cloche.

SLATE SILVERWARE CADDY

This project is a bit time-consuming but very easy. It is a stunning way to incorporate the stark beauty of slate into something useful and elegant.

Materials

BROKEN SLATE

½-GALLON PLASTIC
MILK CONTAINER

Tools

GLUE GUN

· Start with small, deformed, or broken pieces of slate. They all work really well for this project. You can generally find these at your local hardware or building-supply store.

· Cut off the top of a milk jug so the walls are 3 inches high.

· Glue slate pieces around the outside walls and along the inside rim of the jug.

· Fill the caddy with a selection of silverware.

PERFECT CROSTINI

Serves 8

Don't be intimated by crostini: it's just toast in a tuxedo! This recipe is quick, portable, and requires only a few ingredients.

6   TABLESPOONS OLIVE OIL

2   LARGE BAGUETTES

1   TEASPOON COARSE SALT

1. Preheat oven to 350 degrees.

2. Drizzle 2 tablespoons of the olive oil onto a large baking sheet.

3. Slice baguettes crosswise in ½-inch slices and lay slices in a single layer on baking sheet. Drizzle the remaining olive oil over slices. Sprinkle slices evenly with salt and bake until crispy and golden brown, approximately 20–25 minutes.

WARM BLACKBERRY CHUTNEY

Serves 8 (makes approximately 2 cups)

Who knew that making your own fruit spread could be so easy and so delicious? I promise this recipe will not disappoint. And it's a perfect complement to the Perfect Crostini.

2   (16-OUNCE) BAGS FROZEN BLACKBERRIES

1   CUP SUGAR

2   TABLESPOONS FRESH THYME LEAVES (ABOUT 15 SPRIGS), PLUS MORE FOR GARNISH

2   TABLESPOONS LEMON JUICE

1. In a large saucepan, mix the blackberries and sugar. Cook on high heat until fruit defrosts and syrup starts to form, about 15 minutes.

2. Reduce the heat to medium and add thyme. Continue cooking uncovered until mixture thickens, about 20–25 minutes.

3. Remove from heat and add lemon juice. Serve chutney warm, topped with thyme leaves.

MANCHEGO-ARUGULA SALAD WITH POMEGRANATE VINAIGRETTE

Serves 8

I am forever surprised by the great peppery flavor of arugula. Simply pairing it with a fine cheese and a light dressing enhances it perfectly.

Salad

¼ POUND MANCHEGO CHEESE

2 (10-OUNCE) PACKAGES ARUGULA

Vinaigrette

1½ CUPS POMEGRANATE JUICE

¼ TEASPOON DIJON MUSTARD

¼ TEASPOON SUGAR

½ TEASPOON SALT

½ CUP OLIVE OIL

1. For each salad: slice or shave cheese into long, thin strips and lay 3–4 slices on top of approximately 1 cup of the arugula, stacked.

2. For the vinaigrette: in a medium saucepan over high heat, reduce the pomegranate juice until ½ cup remains, about 10 minutes. In a medium bowl, combine the reduced pomegranate juice, mustard, sugar, and salt. Whisk in olive oil in a slow, steady stream. Just before serving, drizzle vinaigrette over salads.

WHITE BEAN–LAMB STEW

Serves 8

Perhaps the recipe I use most from this book, this is a true crowd pleaser and something you can prepare ahead so you can enjoy your party. I often crave the combination of flavors this stew creates.

1	CARROT, PEELED
1	MEDIUM WHITE ONION, PEELED
3	STALKS CELERY, ENDS TRIMMED
5	CLOVES GARLIC, PEELED
½	POUND THICK-SLICED BACON, CUT INTO ½-INCH CHUNKS
2	TABLESPOONS BUTTER
2	TEASPOONS SALT
2½–3 POUNDS LAMB STEW MEAT	
1	(28-OUNCE) CAN DICED TOMATOES
2½	CUPS BEEF BROTH
1	BUNCH MUSTARD GREENS (ABOUT 4 CUPS), COARSELY CHOPPED
4	(13-OUNCE) CANS CANNELLINI BEANS
	SALT AND BLACK PEPPER TO TASTE

1. Puree carrot, onion, celery, and garlic in a food processor. This will be the flavor base for your stew. Set aside.

2. In a medium stockpot over medium-high heat, lightly brown bacon in butter. Sprinkle salt onto lamb and add to bacon. Cook until lamb is browned on all sides, about 10 minutes. Add tomatoes, beef broth, and pureed vegetable mixture, and bring to a boil. Reduce heat to low and simmer uncovered for 1½ hours.

3. Add mustard greens and beans. Return stew to a boil, reduce heat to medium-low, and continue cooking 30 minutes more. Add salt and pepper to taste.

CINNAMON-SUGAR CRISPS
WITH ORANGE CRÈME FRAÎCHE

Serves 8

When we were shooting the photos for this book, it was hard to keep these around long enough to get the shot—that is how good they are! So don't neglect to make this one; and by all means, you may want a little extra dipping sauce.

Crisps

1 (17.3-OUNCE) PACKAGE PUFF
   PASTRY

1 TABLESPOON WATER

3 TABLESPOONS UNSALTED
   BUTTER, MELTED

12 TABLESPOONS CINNAMON

⅓ CUP SUGAR

Crème Fraîche

1 (8-OUNCE) CONTAINER CRÈME
   FRAÎCHE

   JUICE AND ZEST OF 1 ORANGE

2 TABLESPOONS BROWN SUGAR

1. Preheat oven to 425 degrees.

2. For the crisps: defrost puff pastry per directions on package. Unfold one piece of pastry dough. At the center crease, ensure that the sheet is connected by applying a little bit of water with your fingers, making one long piece of dough.

3. Brush top of dough with melted butter and sprinkle evenly with cinnamon and sugar, reserving 2 teaspoons of sugar for later use. Tightly roll dough into a long cylinder and slice roll crosswise into ½-inch rounds. Lay rounds flat on a baking sheet fitted with parchment paper and sprinkle each with ¼ teaspoon sugar. Bake until golden brown and puffed, 18–20 minutes.

4. For the dipping sauce: mix crème fraîche with orange juice and zest. Stir in brown sugar and serve.

CHUNKY APPLE POPOVERS WITH BROWN SUGAR–MASCARPONE CREAM

Serves 8

As you might imagine, these popovers are prettiest when they first come out of the oven, so try to serve them right away. And cream cheese is a great substitute for mascarpone.

Filling

2 TABLESPOONS UNSALTED BUTTER

4 MEDIUM APPLES, PEELED, CORED, AND CUT INTO 8 SLICES EACH

½ CUP BROWN SUGAR

1 TEASPOON CINNAMON

Popovers

2 EGGS

1 CUP MILK

1 CUP FLOUR

½ TEASPOON SALT

1 TEASPOON SUGAR

2 TABLESPOONS UNSALTED BUTTER, MELTED

Cream

1 CUP MASCARPONE

1½ TABLESPOONS BROWN SUGAR

1. For the filling: melt butter in a medium saucepan over medium-high heat. Add apples, brown sugar, and cinnamon, and stir to coat. Cook uncovered until apples are soft but not mushy, 20–25 minutes. Cool.

2. For the popovers: preheat oven to 425 degrees.

3. In a large bowl, whisk eggs and milk together. Add flour, salt, sugar, and butter, and continue to whisk until a smooth batter forms.

4. Grease a muffin tin and fill with 2–3 cooked apple slices per muffin cup. Place in the oven for 5 minutes to heat tin. Remove tin from oven and pour batter over apples to fill cups three-quarters of the way to the top.

5. Bake for 10 minutes at 425 degrees, then reduce temperature to 375 and continue to bake until popovers are golden brown, about 20 minutes.

6. For the cream: while popovers are baking, mix mascarpone and brown sugar. Refrigerate until needed.

7. When popovers are done, remove from tin. Serve with Brown Sugar–Mascarpone Cream.

march
THE WELCOME WAGON

At my sister Marlee's rehearsal dinner, her very best friend from childhood stood up and told the story of how they met. Amy's family had just moved to our neighborhood, and they had barely unpacked when they heard a tiny knock on the door. Amy and her mother opened it to find my wee second-grade sister, wearing white gloves, arms outstretched, offering a loaf of my mother's famous cinnamon bread. It was Sunday, and my sister had just returned from church (hence the white gloves) when my mother ordered her to carry the freshly baked loaf over to our new neighbors. Whenever my mom caught wind of newcomers to the neighborhood, her first friendship strike was to have one of us deliver a loaf of fresh-baked cinnamon bread. Although Marlee is not usually a complainer, this was one job she detested. She had begged my mother not to send her to our new neighbors' home. Little did she know that her delivery that day would start a friendship that would last decades. It is the extraordinary friendship between Amy and Marlee that inspired this chapter. Whether you have a new office mate, sister-in-law, or neighbor, I say extend a white glove and welcome them into your life with all the creativity you can muster.

ADDRESS BAMBOO STEAMERS AND SKEWERS

Look no further than www.pearlriver.com for these inexpensive steamer trays. Use large wacky decorative stamps to give your basic steamers more personality by adding the street address, street name, or family name of that new addition to the neighborhood! Then mix it up—stamp the name on one side and the address on the other side of the skewers.

Materials

BAMBOO STEAMERS

WOODEN SHAPES, SUCH AS
CIRCLES, OVALS, AND TEARDROPS

PACK OF WOODEN SKEWERS

Tools

NUMBERED AND LETTERED
RUBBER STAMPS

RED INK STAMP PAD

GLUE GUN

- For the steamers: stamp the name or street address onto the center of the steamers.

- For the skewers: stamp the name or street number onto the wooden shapes, then hot-glue the shapes to the skewers in different locations and positions near the top half of the skewers.

YOU'VE GOT MAIL

Not only do you have a great cutlery caddy and centerpiece, but your neighbors have a great new personalized mailbox!

Materials

RED VINYL NUMBERS AND LETTERS, ASSORTED SIZES

WHITE MAILBOX

WHITE NAPKINS

ASSORTED RED RIBBON

- Using the vinyl numbers and/or letters, place the street number or family name of your new neighbor on both sides and the front of the mailbox.

- Wrap your cutlery in the napkins and tie with the red ribbon. Pop open the front of the mailbox, stuff in the napkins, and place it by your plates at the buffet table.

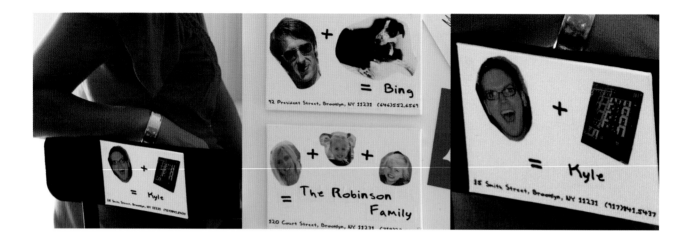

GET-TO-KNOW-YOUR-NEIGHBOR MAGNETS

One of the best things about moving to a new neighborhood is meeting your neighbors. These magnets are a perfect housewarming gift; your new neighbor will know the lay of the land in no time! You can also make this project using plain white magnets from your local craft store—that way, there's no need to place the magnetic tape on the back.

Materials

PICTURES OF NEIGHBORS, THEIR PETS, HOUSES, ETC.

MINI CANVAS BOARDS, 3½ X 5 OR 5 X 7 INCHES

PLAIN WHITE PRINTER PAPER

MOD PODGE (ALL-IN-ONE GLUE, SEALER, AND FINISH)

SELF-ADHESIVE MAGNETIC TAPE

Tools

COLOR PHOTOCOPIER

SMALL SPONGE PAINTBRUSH

· Copy small pictures of your neighbors and useful information about them. We've chosen pictures of pets, children, and houses, but you could go even further and add pictures of their cars, hobbies, or favorite TV shows—anything that will help you introduce the families of the neighborhood. Cut out the pictures.

· On plain white paper, print out useful information about your neighbors in a fun font: their names, addresses, etc. Cut out this information.

· Lay out the information and pictures on the canvas boards (one for each neighbor). Using a small sponge brush and Mod Podge, attach the information to the boards. It might be fun to add mathematical signs, for example, (picture of dog) + (house) = The Brown Family (the neighbor to the left of you).

· Put strips of magnetic tape on the back of the canvas boards at the top and bottom.

PROSCIUTTO AND ASPARAGUS MELTS

Serves 10 (makes 20)

Not too complicated and always a crowd pleaser.

PINCH OF SALT

20 ASPARAGUS TIPS

20 SLICES SKINNY BAGUETTE

OLIVE OIL FOR BRUSHING

20 BITE-SIZE SLICES OF
MOZZARELLA

10 SLICES PROSCIUTTO,
CUT IN HALF

1. Preheat oven to 375 degrees.

2. Blanch asparagus tips in salted boiling water for 20 seconds,
   then drain under cold water or put in ice bath.

3. Brush bread slices with olive oil.

4. Stack asparagus tips on cheese slices, wrap in prosciutto,
   and place on top of bread slices.

5. Brush tops with olive oil and bake until bread is toasted
   and cheese is melted, about 7 minutes.

MARINATED CHICKEN KEBABS WITH LEMON-PEPPER YOGURT SAUCE

Serves 10 (makes 20 kebabs)

If you use regular skewers without decorations, feel free to skewer the chicken before you place it on the grill.

Kebabs

- 2 CUPS EXTRA-VIRGIN OLIVE OIL
- JUICE OF 3 LEMONS
- 3 TABLESPOONS CHOPPED GARLIC
- ¾ TABLESPOONS CHOPPED FRESH ROSEMARY LEAVES (ABOUT 4 SPRIGS)
- ¾ TABLESPOONS FRESH THYME LEAVES (ABOUT 5 SPRIGS)
- 6 SINGLE BONELESS, SKINLESS CHICKEN BREASTS, CLEANED OF FAT AND CUT INTO LARGE CUBES
- SALT AND BLACK PEPPER TO TASTE
- BAMBOO SKEWERS

Sauce

- 2 (7-OUNCE) CONTAINERS PLAIN YOGURT
- 4 TABLESPOONS SOUR CREAM
- 3 TABLESPOONS RED WINE VINEGAR
- ZEST OF 2 LEMONS (FINE)
- JUICE OF 1 LEMON
- 2 TABLESPOONS MINCED GARLIC
- 1 TABLESPOON BLACK PEPPER
- 2 TEASPOONS SALT
- ½ CUP FRESH MINT, CHOPPED (OPTIONAL)

1. For the kebabs: in a plastic bag or airtight container, combine olive oil, lemon juice, garlic, rosemary, and thyme. Add chicken, toss well to coat evenly, and refrigerate overnight.

2. For the sauce, combine all ingredients in a mixing bowl and refrigerate at least 2 hours.

3. Remove chicken pieces from marinade and season well with salt and pepper. Grill chicken for 5 minutes on each side, until golden brown and juices of chicken run clear when pricked with the end of a skewer. Thread 3 pieces of chicken onto each skewer. Serve with Lemon-Pepper Yogurt Sauce.

BIBB WRAPS WITH ORZO SALAD

Serves 10 (makes approximately 20 lettuce wraps)

Encourage your guests to eat the lettuce wraps with their fingers, the way you would your basic spring roll.

3 CUPS WATER

2 CUPS ORZO

4 TABLESPOONS EXTRA-VIRGIN
   OLIVE OIL

½ CUP PINE NUTS

1 CLOVE GARLIC

¾ CUP FRESH PARSLEY LEAVES

   JUICE OF 2 LEMONS

½ CUP DRIED APRICOTS

½ CUP THINLY SLICED SCALLION

20 BIBB LETTUCE LEAVES
   (2–3 HEADS)

   SALT AND BLACK PEPPER
   TO TASTE

1. In a small saucepan, bring lightly salted water to a boil. Add orzo and cook until soft, 8–10 minutes. Drain in a colander and rinse with cold water until cool. Place orzo in a bowl.

2. In a small sauté pan, toast pine nuts with 1 teaspoon of the olive oil over medium heat until golden brown, stirring often. Set aside to cool.

3. In a food processor, pulse garlic and parsley until well chopped. Add lemon juice and apricots. Pulse until apricots are in small chunks.

4. Remove mixture from processor and combine in bowl with orzo. Add scallions, the remaining olive oil, pine nuts, salt, and pepper, and mix together.

5. Fill the center of each bibb leaf with a spoonful of orzo salad and serve.

CUCUMBER SALAD WITH MARINATED RED ONION AND FRESH HERBS

Serves 10

Hothouse cucumbers are best for this salad because they have more flesh and fewer seeds. They also have a thinner, less-waxy skin and tend to be a little crisper than your average cucumber.

Marinade

1   CUP SUGAR

1   CUP RED WINE VINEGAR

1   CUP WATER OR OLIVE OIL

2   LARGE RED ONIONS, SLICED THIN

Salad

3   CUCUMBERS

¼   CUP OLIVE OIL

    JUICE OF 2 LEMONS

½   CUP FRESH DILL LEAVES

    SALT AND BLACK PEPPER
    TO TASTE

1. For the marinade: combine sugar, vinegar, and water in a glass or plastic bowl and mix to combine. Add onions and cover with plastic. Marinate in refrigerator overnight.

2. For the salad: slice cucumbers in half, remove seeds, and thinly slice into half-moon shapes. In a large bowl, combine cucumbers, olive oil, lemon juice, dill, and onion marinade. Season to taste with salt and pepper.

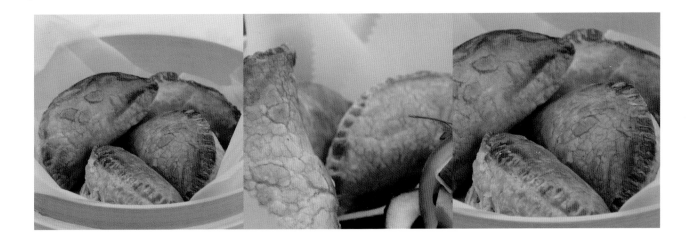

HERBED FETA PUFFS

Serves 10–12 (makes approximately 24)

Using premade puff pastry makes these bite-size delights simple and easy.

½ (7-OUNCE) PACKAGE CREAM
  CHEESE

½ (8-OUNCE) PACKAGE FETA
  CHEESE

3 SCALLIONS

¼ CUP FRESH MINT LEAVES

  SALT AND PEPPER TO TASTE

1 EGG YOLK

1 TABLESPOON HEAVY CREAM

2 PACKAGES PUFF PASTRY

1. In a food processor, combine cream cheese, feta cheese, scallions, mint, salt, and pepper, and purée until herbs and cheese are well blended. Refrigerate at least 1 hour.

2. Preheat oven to 375 degrees.

3. Make an egg wash by whisking together egg yolk, cream, and salt.

4. Defrost puff pastry per directions on package. Using a cookie cutter or cup, cut 10–12 circles into the puff pastry dough (about the size of the palm of your hand). Place a dollop of cheese mixture in the center of each circle. With a brush, paint the outer rim with egg wash. Fold the circle in half and seal the outside rim by pressing with a fork.

5. Place puffs on a greased sheet tray and brush tops with egg wash. Bake until golden brown, 20–25 minutes.

CHOCOLATE-SPICE CAKE   *Makes one 10-inch-round cake*

This unusual cake is dense with flavor.

NONSTICK COOKING SPRAY

8   OUNCES BITTERSWEET BAKER'S
    CHOCOLATE, CHOPPED

1¼ CUPS ALL-PURPOSE FLOUR

1   TEASPOON BAKING POWDER

1   TEASPOON BAKING SODA

3   EGG YOLKS

1¼ CUPS SUGAR

1   CUP VEGETABLE OIL

1½ TEASPOONS CINNAMON

¼   TEASPOON CAYENNE PEPPER

½   TEASPOON GROUND GINGER

½   TEASPOON SALT

4   EGG WHITES

    CONFECTIONERS' SUGAR FOR
    DUSTING

1. Preheat oven to 350 degrees. Lightly spray 10-inch-round cake pan with nonstick spray.

2. Place chocolate in a large food processor with flour, baking powder, and baking soda. Pulse mixture until combined and chocolate is finely chopped.

3. In a mixing bowl, beat egg yolks and half of the sugar with an electric mixer until pale. Reduce speed and add oil slowly. Add cinnamon, cayenne, ginger, and salt, and mix until combined. Add chocolate mixture to bowl.

4. In a separate mixing bowl, beat egg whites until frothy. Add the remaining sugar and beat until medium peaks form. Mix a third of egg whites into the chocolate mixture, then gently fold in the remainder.

5. Pour batter into pan and spread evenly. Bake until the sides pull away from the pan and a toothpick inserted in the middle comes out clean, about 40 minutes. Allow cake to cool, remove from pan, and dust with confectioners' sugar.

Tabletop
YIKES, STRIPES! TABLETOP

LANTERN PIÑATAS

BIRTHDAY PENNANT

Menu
POPCORN GRAB BAGS

PIZZA STICK ROLL-UPS

PB & J FRENCH TOAST ROLL-UPS

CANDY PEAS

BROWNIE PUDDING POPS

WAFER CAKE

april
KIDS' DAY

To say my daughter's birthday is a big deal for me is a giant understatement. Not only do I love celebrating her birth, I also love putting on an all-kids party. But this year, for her third birthday party, I struggled a bit. She was just starting to get into pink and princesses, which seemed a bit unoriginal. Then there were characters like Elmo and Dora, but I had been to more than one party where the creatures scared the kids, which was not the festive mood I was looking for. What to do? Then it came to me. For the perfect kids' bash, I had to look no further than my old standby: color. Why not embrace color and mix it up a bit with some stripes? Yellow was one of Prentiss's favorite colors, and I could compliment it with some greens and purples in the form of striping. I love to throw parties where the second the guests (in this case toddlers) enter, they let out gasps of delight. Between a bright pennant banner, colorful homemade piñatas, a striped tabletop, and yummy treats, the little ones were delightfully wowed. So for your next child's birthday, I encourage you to skip the commercial standbys and simply use colors, shapes, and creativity to ring in your wee one's special day.

YIKES, STRIPES! TABLETOP

We've chosen yellow, green, and purple for this tabletop, but feel free to customize this party with your child's favorite colors. And don't worry about the kids making a mess—colored duct tape resists wear and wipes up easily.

Materials

LONG WOODEN BOARD

YELLOW, GREEN, AND PURPLE DUCT
TAPE IN VARYING WIDTHS

2 BUCKETS

Tools

SCISSORS

- Stripe the board with a variety of colored tapes, varying the widths of both your tape strips and their placement on the board.
- Place the board on top of the buckets to form a table.

LANTERN PIÑATAS

I had my first piñata party when I was eleven (very exotic for a small town in Michigan). I was so excited at the thought of whacking a piñata that I spent all morning before the party collecting sticks and hand-painting them for my friends. A great way to include this fun game at a smaller child's party without the whacking is to let the kids simply tug on ribbons to get their prizes.

Materials

12 BUBBLE LANTERNS
(1 FOR EACH CHILD)

RIBBON

TAPE

TOYS AND CANDY

Tools

SCISSORS

· For each lantern: cut two 4-foot sections of ribbon, and tape one end of each ribbon inside the opening of the lantern. This will create two tails that the kids can grab onto and pull, forcing all the goodies to come out.

· Fill the lantern with toys and treats.

· To hang the lantern, thread another ribbon through the wire in the top and suspend it from the ceiling or a tree.

BIRTHDAY PENNANT

Boy or girl, these sports-inspired birthday pennants are perfect for anyone's birthday bash. Customize them with your little one's favorite colors. You're sure to be a winner with these decorations!

Materials

3–4 YARDS YELLOW COTTON FABRIC

PURPLE IRON-ON SPORTS
NUMBERS AND LETTERS

PURPLE AND GREEN TAPE

PURPLE RIBBON

Tools

PINKING SHEARS

RULER

IRON

- Measure four two-by-three-foot triangles and cut out of fabric with pinking shears.

- Using the numbers and letters, spell out your child's name, age, and any festive message on the triangles. Iron them into place.

- Tape stripes above and below the numbers and letters.

- Fold over the tops of the triangles and tape them down to create sleeves for the ribbon.

- String the ribbon through the sleeves, hang the pennants from tree branches, and watch them ripple in the breeze.

POPCORN GRAB BAGS

Serves 12

A great way to get the kids involved with this fun activity is to have them help mix and stir. Here are three flavor combinations that we think will really capture their imagination.

4   BAGS BUTTERED MICROWAVE
    POPCORN, POPPED

12 SMALL PAPER BAGS

Malted Mix-In

1   CUP MALTED MILK

2   CUPS SHELLED SUNFLOWER
    SEEDS

2   TABLESPOONS SEASONING SALT

Marshmallow Mix-In

1   BAG MINI MARSHMALLOWS

2   CUPS M&M'S

½   CUP SHELLED PEANUTS

CinnaSugar Mix-In

1   CUP GRANULATED SUGAR

¼   CUP CINNAMON

1. Combine any of the three mix-in combinations in a medium bowl.

2. Fill each paper bag with a few handfuls of popcorn. Add mix-ins, shake, and eat!

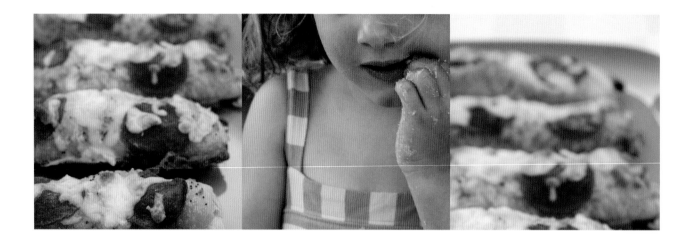

PIZZA STICK ROLL-UPS

Serves 12

A no-mess way for kids to enjoy pizza!

3 (13.8-OUNCE) CANS
REFRIGERATED PIZZA DOUGH

1 CUP PIZZA SAUCE

4 CUPS SHREDDED MOZZARELLA
CHEESE

15 FRESH BASIL LEAVES, CHOPPED

1 (8-OUNCE) PACKAGE PEPPERONI
SLICES

SESAME AND POPPY SEEDS

1. Preheat oven to 350 degrees.

2. Open and unroll 1 of the cans of the pizza dough and cut
dough into 4 even squares. Spread a third of the sauce on
the squares and sprinkle with a third of the cheese and
basil. Fold square in half, making a pocket; press the seam
to secure. Fold the ends under as well, so cheese does not
bake out of rolls.

3. Place rolls seam side down on a baking sheet. Repeat with
the second and third cans of the dough. Top rolls with your
choice of poppy or sesame seeds, additional cheese, pepperoni, or all of the above!

4. Bake rolls until golden brown, 20–25 minutes.

PB & J FRENCH TOAST ROLL-UPS

Serves 12

I first made this dish for my television show on the A&E network. Since then it has been my most re-quested recipe for kids. So get rolling!

12 SLICES BREAD

1 (18-OUNCE) JAR PEANUT BUTTER

1 (12-OUNCE) JAR JELLY

5 EGGS

½ CUP MILK

2 TEASPOONS VANILLA

4 TABLESPOONS BUTTER

  POWDERED SUGAR FOR DUSTING

1. Remove crusts from bread and spread one half of each slice with peanut butter, the other with jelly. Roll bread, beginning with jelly end.

2. In a medium bowl, mix eggs, milk, and vanilla. Dip each roll into egg mixture to coat. Let excess drip off.

3. Heat a large griddle or skillet to medium-high heat and melt butter. Cook rolls until golden brown.

4. Place rolls on a serving dish and dust with powdered sugar.

CANDY PEAS

Serves 12

The children will eat their peas and perhaps even mind their Q's when you mix them with a bit of honey and cinnamon.

3 (10-OUNCE) BOXES FROZEN PEAS

½ CUP WATER

1 TEASPOON SALT

½ CUP HONEY

¼ TEASPOON CINNAMON

1. Place frozen peas, water, and salt in a medium saucepan over high heat. Cook until peas are thawed, about 5 minutes. Drain peas and place in a bowl.

2. In the same saucepan, combine honey and cinnamon, and melt over medium heat for 3–4 minutes. Pour over peas and stir to combine.

3. Chill peas in refrigerator until ready to serve.

BROWNIE PUDDING POPS

Serves 12

Who knew you could put brownie and pudding mixes on a stick?

1 BOX FUDGE BROWNIE MIX

13 PAPER (3-OUNCE) CUPS

2 (4-SERVING-SIZE) PACKAGES
   WHITE CHOCOLATE- OR
   VANILLA-FLAVOR JELL-O
   INSTANT PUDDING MIX

2 CUPS COLD MILK

   NONSTICK COOKING SPRAY

6 POPSICLE STICKS, CUT IN HALF

1. Preheat oven to 350 degrees.

2. Prepare brownies as directed on box and bake in a
   9 x 12-inch pan. Once cooled, use one of the paper cups
   to cut 24 circles out of brownies. Set circles aside.

3. In a medium bowl, whisk pudding mix and milk together.
   Continue whisking for 2 minutes. Set aside.

4. Grease 12 of the paper cups and fill each with 1 brownie
   round. Top each with 1–2 tablespoons of the pudding.
   Place a second brownie round on top of pudding. Insert
   a Popsicle stick in the center of each and put in the freezer
   until frozen, 6–8 hours.

5. When ready to serve, cut cups away from pops with scissors.

WAFER CAKE

Serves 12 (makes one 2-tier cake)

The simple addition of these colorful dots will make it look as if you have hints of professional cake-decorating ability. This cake is the perfect addition to a small child's birthday celebration!

Cake

- 2 (2-LAYER-SIZE) PACKAGES CAKE MIX
- 4 (16-OUNCE) TUBS PREPARED FROSTING

Wafers

- 1 (1-POUND) BAG CONFECTIONERS' SUGAR
- 6 TABLESPOONS WATER
  ASSORTED FOOD COLORING
  35-PLUS NILLA WAFERS

1. For the cake: prepare one of the packages of cake batter as per instructions on box and pour batter into a greased 9 x 2-inch round cake pan. Bake until a toothpick inserted in the center comes out clean, 45–50 minutes.

2. Repeat process with the second package of cake mix, but bake in an 8 x 2-inch round cake pan.

3. For the wafers: while cakes are baking, mix confectioners' sugar and water in a medium bowl until a thick paste forms. Divide paste into 3 equal parts and put in 3 separate bowls. Mix in food coloring, using colors of your choice. Once desired color is achieved, add an additional 2–4 teaspoons of water to each icing mixture to make them easily pourable.

4. Place wafers on a rack over a baking sheet (to catch the runoff). Pour icing over cookies until fully covered. Let sit until icing has hardened, 5–10 minutes.

5. Stack 8-inch cake on top of 9-inch cake, and cover both cake tiers with frosting of your choice, then stick colored wafers to sides.

Tabletop

CORKSCREW NAPKIN RINGS

PRETTY LITTLE PICTURE

REMNANT TABLECLOTH

Menu

GREEN GARDEN SOUP

PARMESAN-CAYENNE SCONES

STACKED SALAD WITH AVOCADO DRESSING

DEEP-DISH COUNTRY QUICHE

LEMON-RHUBARB TRIFLE

POKE CUPCAKES

may
FEMININE FETE

It is the mother of all months, the month that features that all-important celebration: Mother's Day. I love this day, first because I am a mother and second because I love spoiling my own mother. My mom, who we refer to as Mother Meg, has many a favorite thing. She has never met a bubble bath she did not like. Chocolate is an all-time love. Tea is constantly on the ready, and oh how she sighs breathlessly when presented with an iris or a lilac in her favorite color—purple. I believe that you should fight the urge to use Mother's Day as an opportunity to give your mother what *you* think she should have (those pants that make her look racy, curtains to replace whatever those things are on her window, your favorite scented candle) and instead gather a few of *her* absolute favorite things. It is the perfect day to prove to your number one caretaker that she is the one who knows best, and that yes, in fact you have paid attention to the things that make her smile bright. So I say use the following pages as a blueprint or outline to plug in your mother's favorites. I used a collection of purple fabric to adorn the table, but be inspired to use your mom's favorite color instead. The simple frame vases will highlight any mother's favorite flower, and of course any cooking that she does not have to do will make her day. And remember that sometimes the best gift you can give a busy lady is as simple as time—especially girl time. So be sure to assemble a formidable feminine posse to help her indulge in her big day. Female fetes are also great ways to revel in all things that are strictly feminine, like being a bride or having a baby. So come on—glorify the girly and take this time to celebrate with all of the wonderful women in your life.

CORKSCREW NAPKIN RINGS

I am a big fan of maypoles; obviously, they are far too big for a tabletop, so this is a smaller version that wraps all the colored ribbon and flowers into a whimsical napkin ring. And I firmly believe you can never have too many silk flowers! Grab a bundle every time you see them on sale, and you'll have a variety to choose from for projects like this.

Materials

ARMATURE WIRE

GREEN FLORAL TAPE

RIBBON

SILK FLOWERS

Tools

GLUE GUN

SCISSORS

- Cut the wire into 12-inch sections (one per napkin ring).

- Curl the wires into corkscrew shapes.

- Glue flowers at the end of each wire corkscrew.

- Starting at one end, glue ribbon and floral tape to the corkscrew. Continue wrapping the corkscrew by alternately weaving the ribbon over and under the floral tape until the entire corkscrew is covered. Periodically weave in small flowers and leaves.

PRETTY LITTLE PICTURE

At the Katie Brown Workshop, we are always looking for new ways to show off a simple flower—and this is one of our favorites!

Materials

DEEP WOODEN PICTURE FRAME

CEILING SCREW OR LARGE
EYELET SCREW

PLASTIC FLORAL BEAKER

ASSORTED FLOWERS

· Remove the glass and backing from the frame.

· Mark appropriate placement for the screw inside the frame, ensuring that your beaker (and flower) will fit inside the frame.

· Screw the screw into the frame and place the beaker in the eyelet.

· Insert flowers into the beaker.

REMNANT TABLECLOTH

One of my favorite objects growing up was a box that my mom had full of fabric remnants. Oh, the creations I made from the fabric in that box! I like to think of this project as perhaps a more sophisticated use of fantastic fabric pieces, and one that will surely make any tabletop a gorgeous centerpiece to your shower. If you run out of fabric pieces, reuse old tablecloths, sheets, or clothing. Can't find long enough strips? Attach two pieces of the same width.

Materials

ASSORTMENT OF PURPLE FABRIC

ASSORTMENT OF PURPLE RIBBON

1 TUBE CLEAR-DRYING WASHABLE FABRIC GLUE

Tools

SCISSORS

RULER

- Measure the dimensions of the tabletop.

- Make the dimensions of the finished tablecloth 2 feet longer and wider than the tabletop.

- Tear the fabric into long strips the length of the tablecloth.

- Use fabric glue to adhere strips of fabric and ribbon together, each strip overlapping the previous.

- Cut the ends to make them as even as possible.

GREEN GARDEN SOUP

Serves 16

This soup calls for more ingredients than my usual recipes, but I promise every one is worth it.

4 TABLESPOONS BUTTER

2 MEDIUM ONIONS, CHOPPED

4 CLOVES GARLIC, CHOPPED

2 CUCUMBERS, PEELED, SEEDED, AND CHOPPED

2 (13-OUNCE) CANS ARTICHOKES, CHOPPED

8 GREEN ONIONS, CHOPPED

2 BUNCHES ASPARAGUS, CHOPPED

1 POUND CHICKEN TENDERS, CUT INTO SMALL CHUNKS

2 (10-OUNCE) PACKAGES BUTTON MUSHROOMS, QUARTERED

6 CUPS CHICKEN BROTH

4 TABLESPOONS LEMON JUICE

3 CUPS HEAVY CREAM

SALT AND BLACK PEPPER TO TASTE

1. In a large stockpot, melt butter over medium-high heat. Add onions, garlic, cucumbers, artichokes, green onions, and asparagus. Cook until soft, about 20 minutes. Add chicken, mushrooms, and broth, and bring to a boil. Reduce heat and cook for another 20 minutes.

2. Remove soup from heat and add lemon juice and half of the cream. In batches, puree soup mixture in blender until smooth. Add soup back to pot. Return to a boil to warm through, and stir in the remaining cream. Add salt and pepper to taste.

PARMESAN-CAYENNE SCONES

Serves 16 (makes 32)

I have never tasted anything with buttermilk I did not like. Add a pinch of cayenne, and it can't be beat!

6 CUPS FLOUR

6 TEASPOONS BAKING POWDER

5 TEASPOONS SALT

1 TEASPOON COARSE BLACK PEPPER

2 TABLESPOONS CAYENNE PEPPER

1 CUP COLD BUTTER, CUT INTO SQUARES

4 CUPS GRATED PARMESAN CHEESE

2 CUPS MILK

1 CUP BUTTERMILK

4 EGGS

1. Preheat oven to 350 degrees.

2. In the bowl of a food processor, combine flour, baking powder, salt, black pepper, and cayenne pepper. Add butter and pulse until mixture resembles fine crumbs. Pour dough into a large bowl and stir in Parmesan, making sure it is evenly distributed.

3. In a separate bowl, whisk together milk, buttermilk, and eggs. Add to flour mixture and stir until combined. Knead once or twice to bring it all together. If dough is too sticky, sprinkle on more flour. Divide dough into your favorite small molds.

4. Bake until slightly golden, 20–25 minutes. Serve warm.

STACKED SALAD
WITH AVOCADO DRESSING

Serves 16

This is one of those salads that looks a lot harder to make than it truly is, so be prepared for your guests to be impressed.

Salad

2   GRANNY SMITH APPLES, CORED

1   LARGE RED ONION, PEELED

8   CUPS MÂCHE (LAMB'S LETTUCE)
    OR OTHER BABY GREENS

8   CUPS CHOPPED FRISÉE

⅔   CUP CHOPPED WALNUTS

32 SLICES SPECK (SMOKED
    PROSCIUTTO)

8   GREEN ONIONS, GREEN PARTS
    THINLY SLICED

Dressing

1   AVOCADO, PEELED AND CUBED

1   TABLESPOON LEMON JUICE

1   TABLESPOON RANCH DRESSING MIX

1   CUP BUTTERMILK

½   CUP CREAM

1   TEASPOON SALT

½   TEASPOON PEPPER

1. For the salad: using a food processor, thinly slice apples.

2. Do the same with the red onion.

3. Mix the mâche and frisée together and place 1 cup of the greens on each salad plate. Top each serving with 3–4 apple slices and a few slices of the red onion. Sprinkle with ½ teaspoon of the walnuts.

4. Roll two slices of speck and cut crosswise to make ribbons (chiffonade) for each salad. Pile loosely on top of red onions. Sprinkle with green onions. Serve with Avocado Dressing on the side.

5. For the dressing: place all ingredients in a blender. Blend on high until smooth. If dressing is too thick, add a little water to thin.

DEEP-DISH COUNTRY QUICHE

Serves 16 (makes 2)

I really like this version of the classic quiche. This deep-dish variation offers your guests a hearty portion that will satisfy their tastebuds and their appetite.

3	TABLESPOONS BUTTER
4	SLICES THICK-CUT SMOKED BACON, CUBED
2	LARGE ONIONS, SLICED
2	DEEP-DISH PIE CRUSTS
2	CUPS HALVED CHERRY TOMATOES
2	(6-OUNCE) PACKAGES GOAT CHEESE
2	CUPS WATERCRESS
16	EGGS
1½	CUPS MILK
4	TEASPOONS SALT
2	TEASPOONS PEPPER

1. Preheat oven to 350 degrees.

2. Melt butter in a medium saucepan and add bacon. Cook on medium heat until bacon is slightly browned. Add onions and continue to cook until soft, about 15 minutes.

3. Divide onion-bacon mixture evenly between two pie crusts. Do the same with cherry tomatoes, goat cheese, and watercress.

4. In a large bowl, whisk together eggs, milk, salt, and pepper. Divide mixture and pour into pie crusts.

5. Bake quiches until centers are set and tops are golden brown, 50–55 minutes.

LEMON-RHUBARB TRIFLE

Serves 16

So fancy, so pretty, and sooo good!

8 (12-INCH-LONG) STALKS RHUBARB

½ CUP SUGAR

4 (4-SERVING-SIZE) PACKAGES
   LEMON-FLAVOR JELL-O INSTANT PUDDING MIX

8 CUPS COLD MILK

2 SPONGE CAKES, CUT INTO SMALL CUBES

4 (8-OUNCE) CONTAINERS COOL WHIP TOPPING

1. Preheat oven to 400 degrees.

2. Cut rhubarb into 2-inch chunks and place on a baking sheet
   fitted with parchment paper. Sprinkle with 2 tablespoons
   of the sugar and bake until soft, 20–25 minutes. Let cool.

3. When rhubarb has cooled, place in a bowl and stir in the
   remaining sugar.

4. In a large bowl, combine pudding mix and milk. Whisk for
   2 minutes and let set in refrigerator for 5 minutes.

5. In 16 individual glasses, layer pudding, rhubarb puree,
   cake pieces, and Cool Whip. Repeat and top each with a dollop of Cool Whip.

POKE CUPCAKES

Serves 24

*It is just so fun to see what happens when you add Jell-O to these
cupcakes—it gives a touch of color and texture that will delight
your guests.*

1 (2-LAYER-SIZE) PACKAGE WHITE CAKE MIX

1 CUP BOILING WATER

1 (4-SERVING-SIZE) PACKAGE JELL-O FLAVORED GELATIN, ANY RED FLAVOR

1 (8-OUNCE) CONTAINER COOL WHIP TOPPING

1. Prepare cake batter and bake as directed on package for
   24 cupcakes. Cool in pans 10 minutes. Pierce cupcakes
   with large fork at ¼-inch intervals.

2. Stir boiling water into dry Jell-O mix until completely
   dissolved. Spoon liquid evenly over cupcakes. Refrigerate
   30 minutes. Remove cupcakes from pans.

3. Place a dollop of Cool Whip on top of each cupcake.

june
SPICY GRADUATION
CELEBRATION

One of the best parts of my job is all the young, talented people I get to work with. We brainstorm, craft, and play around in what I refer to as a "romper room for grown-ups." It's truly amazing to watch them navigate on the computer, experience their burgeoning confidence in the workplace, and hear about their many world travels. These experiences will undoubtedly lead to extraordinary things, and I am grateful I get to catch a glimpse of them. In a time when young people have so many opportunities and experiences, how do we keep them engaged and motivated? I propose sending your emerging adult into the "real" world with a graduation party inspired by faraway lands. Muddy reds and, deep oranges, different spices and delicacies, are a great way to embrace their flourishing curiosity. Not to mention that you yourself will appear to be an expert explorer of sorts, which enhances your clout. So whether you have a graduating daughter, coworker, or nephew, send them off with a party that celebrates the open exploration they are surely about to experience.

SPICY INVITATIONS

This is a fun play on the idea of a message in a bottle. . . . You may even want to include details about the graduation or the graduate.

Materials

LARGE JAR OF MOROCCAN SPICE BLEND

SMALL JARS WITH CORK TOPS (1 FOR EACH INVITATION)

8½ X 11-INCH ORANGE PAPER

THIN LEATHER LACE

GLUE STICKS

Tools

SCISSORS

GLUE GUN

PEN

SMALL HOLE PUNCH

· Fill your small spice jars with your favorite Moroccan spice blend.

· Print or write your invitations on strips of orange paper the width of the spice jars.

· Glue one end of each invitation around each jar.

· Punch a hole in the other end of the invitations and thread the holes with leather lace.

· Roll the invitations around the jars and tie with the leather lace.

· Place the jars in padded envelopes, address, stamp, and send.

MOROCCAN COASTERS

Stencil paste was a great new discovery for us at the Katie Brown Workshop. The three-dimensional effect and texture are just right for this exotic tabletop. Try www.stencilease.com if you're having problems finding that perfect stencil.

Materials

4-INCH-SQUARE TILES
(1 FOR EACH COASTER)

MOROCCAN-THEMED STENCIL

STENCIL PASTE

ORANGE PAINT

CLEAR SHELLAC

Tools

PUTTY KNIFE

SPRAY ADHESIVE

PAINTBRUSH

· For each coaster, spray the back of the stencil with spray adhesive and position it on a tile.

· Mix the stencil paste and acrylic paint, tinting to the preferred shade of orange.

· Apply the paste-paint mixture to the stencil with a putty knife.

· Remove the stencil and allow the paste to dry.

· Cover the entire coaster with a coat of shellac.

SPARKLING STICKS

This is such a cool way to incorporate your theme into your tabletop. And there are never-ending ways you can combine and configure your varying pieces of gem-encrusted trim.

Materials

WOOD TRIM

ORANGE PAINT

PLASTIC JEWELS IN VARYING
SHADES OF ORANGE AND RED

GLASS PIECES

Tools

SMALL SAW

PAINTBRUSH

GLUE GUN

· Cut the trim to varying lengths with the saw.

· Paint all the pieces of trim orange.

· Glue jewels and glass to the trim.

· Arrange the pieces on your table in a pattern, radiating from the center.

HONEY-SPICED ALMONDS

Serves 10

I will never forget when I started my catering company and offered sweet and spicy peanuts as one of the gift items. I had to toss peanuts for days, but they were delicious! Although I don't suggest that you mix quite as many as I did in the early years of my career, I do suggest you toss a few of these delights for the occasion.

2 TABLESPOONS OLIVE OIL

6 CUPS WHOLE BLANCHED
   ALMONDS

⅓ CUP HONEY

2 TEASPOONS SMOKED PAPRIKA

2 TEASPOONS CINNAMON

2 TEASPOONS CUMIN

2 TEASPOONS CAYENNE

2 TABLESPOONS SALT

4 TABLESPOONS SESAME SEEDS

1. Preheat oven to 300 degrees.

2. Heat a large sauté pan on high and add olive oil. Add almonds to pan, toast for 1 minute, stirring often, and reduce heat to low. Continue to stir until the almonds are light golden brown, 6–7 minutes. Add honey, spices, salt, and sesame seeds, and stir to coat evenly.

3. Spread nuts out evenly on a large sheet tray and place in the oven until honey is dry, 10–15 minutes. Allow nuts to cool before serving.

HUMMUS

If you're short on time, buy your favorite toppings at the store, but always make the hummus yourself. You'll see that hummus really is much better homemade, and much less expensive. And you can make it several days in advance.

2–3 CLOVES GARLIC, ROUGHLY CHOPPED

3 (15½-OUNCE) CANS CHICKPEAS

1½ CUPS TAHINI PASTE

1½ TABLESPOONS SALT

½ CUP LEMON JUICE

½ CUP WATER

½ CUP EXTRA-VIRGIN OLIVE OIL, PLUS EXTRA FOR DRIZZLING

PAPRIKA FOR GARNISH

⅓ CUP SLICED SCALLIONS FOR GARNISH

1. In the bowl of a food processor, combine garlic, chickpeas, tahini paste, and salt, and pulse 3–4 times. Scrape down sides of bowl and add lemon juice and water. Puree until smooth, scraping down sides as needed.

2. When mixture is smooth in consistency, add olive oil and pulse until well combined.

3. Keep hummus in an airtight container in the refrigerator until ready for use.

Olive Tapenade Topping

1 CUP PACKED FRESH PARSLEY LEAVES

1 SMALL SHALLOT, COARSELY CHOPPED

1 TABLESPOON LEMON JUICE

3 TABLESPOONS CAPERS

1½ CUPS PITTED KALAMATA OLIVES

4 TABLESPOONS OLIVE OIL

SALT AND BLACK PEPPER TO TASTE

In a food processor, chop parsley and shallot with lemon juice. Add capers, olives, and olive oil, and pulse to rough chop. Season with salt and pepper, and reserve.

Roasted Red Pepper Puree Topping

1 SMALL SHALLOT, COARSELY CHOPPED

2 TABLESPOONS LEMON JUICE

1 (14-OUNCE) JAR ROASTED RED PEPPERS, COARSELY CHOPPED

4 TABLESPOONS EXTRA-VIRGIN OLIVE OIL

SALT AND BLACK PEPPER TO TASTE

In a food processor, chop shallot with lemon juice. Add red peppers and olive oil; pulse until pureed but still a bit chunky. Season to taste with salt and pepper.

Roasted Garlic Topping

3 SMALL HEADS OF GARLIC

3 TABLESPOONS OLIVE OIL

SALT TO TASTE

1. Preheat oven to 400 degrees.

2. Cut off one end of each garlic head and place on foil square. Pour olive oil over tops, season with salt, and wrap each individually. Bake garlic until completely soft, about 45 minutes.

3. Allow to cool, then remove garlic from foil and separate heads into individual cloves. Squeeze out center of each clove.

For Service

1. Divide hummus into three mounds, either in separate bowls or on one large serving platter. Create a well in the center of each with the back of a spoon. Fill each well with one of the toppings.

2. For garnish: drizzle hummus mounds with olive oil, sprinkle with paprika, and scatter with scallions. Serve with pita bread.

MOROCCAN CARROT SALAD

Serves 10

These sweet and spicy carrots add just the right zip to your meal.

6   CUPS SHREDDED CARROTS

½   CUP RAISINS

½   CUP GOLDEN RAISINS

3–4 ORANGES, PEELED AND
      SECTIONED (ABOUT 2½ CUPS)

1   TABLESPOON HONEY

1¼ TEASPOONS CUMIN

½   TEASPOON SMOKED (OR
      REGULAR) PAPRIKA

⅛   TEASPOON CAYENNE PEPPER

1½ CUPS THINLY SLICED
      SCALLIONS

1   CUP CILANTRO LEAVES

      JUICE OF 2 LEMONS

⅓   CUP EXTRA-VIRGIN OLIVE OIL

      SALT TO TASTE

In a large mixing bowl, combine all ingredients except salt, toss well, and refrigerate for at least 1 hour to marry flavors. Add salt to taste before serving.

MOROCCAN BRAISED CHICKEN

Serves 10

When my chef collaborator Kaegan Welch came up with this dish, all work stopped in the Workshop; the aroma was intoxicating, and the flavor did not disappoint!

¼ CUP OLIVE OIL

10 CHICKEN THIGHS

10 CHICKEN DRUMSTICKS

SALT TO TASTE

1¾ TEASPOONS TURMERIC

1¼ TEASPOONS PAPRIKA

¾ TEASPOON CAYENNE PEPPER

3 ONIONS, SLICED

9 CLOVES GARLIC, CRUSHED

2 STRIPS ORANGE PEEL

2 STRIPS LEMON PEEL

1½ CINNAMON STICKS

2 CANS PITTED BLACK OLIVES

3 TABLESPOONS HONEY

1½ CUPS PITTED AND CHOPPED DATES

6 CUPS CHICKEN STOCK

1. Preheat oven to 350 degrees.

2. Heat a large saucepan or Dutch oven on high and add olive oil. Season chicken on all sides with salt and rub dry spices onto chicken. When pan is smoking hot, add chicken, skin side down, and sauté on all sides until golden. Sear chicken in small batches for best results. Do not cook chicken all the way through; only brown the outside.

3. Remove chicken from pan and add onions and garlic. Lower heat to medium and sweat until onions are soft, about 5 minutes. Add orange peel, lemon peel, and cinnamon sticks. Stir mixture and sauté for an additional 1–2 minutes.

4. Add olives, honey, and dates. Arrange chicken pieces on top in one layer, pour chicken stock halfway up sides of chicken, and bring liquid to a simmer. Cover pot and place in oven until chicken is tender, about 1 hour. Add salt to taste.

SCALLION-MINT COUSCOUS

Serves 10

This is just what you need to accompany the very flavorful Moroccan chicken dish.

6   CUPS WATER

1   STICK BUTTER

1   TABLESPOON SALT

2   CINNAMON STICKS

3   (10-OUNCE) BOXES PLAIN
     COUSCOUS

1½ CUPS SLICED SCALLIONS

½   CUP FRESH MINT LEAVES,
     CHOPPED

1. In a large saucepan, bring water, butter, salt, and cinnamon to a boil. Add couscous, stir, cover, remove from heat, and let sit for five minutes.

2. Add scallions and fluff couscous with a fork. Place in a serving dish and garnish with chopped mint.

SESAME-HONEY CAKES

Serves 10 (makes 20 cakes)

I was demonstrating this recipe at our church holiday fair when someone watching pointed out that it is, in fact, a very Greek-inspired dessert. Although this news was Greek to me, the fact that this recipe is so simple, so quick, and so delicious is not!

6   CUPS VEGETABLE OIL

2   CUPS HONEY

2   (7.5-OUNCE) CANS
     REFRIGERATED BISCUIT DOUGH

⅓   CUP TOASTED SESAME SEEDS

1. In a large saucepan, heat oil over medium flame. Heat honey in a small saucepan.

2. Remove biscuits from can and form into 20 balls. Fry balls in oil, in batches, until golden brown, about 2 minutes per side.

3. Remove cakes to cooling rack or paper towel and pat dry. Dip each into the hot honey, coating evenly, remove to cooling rack, and sprinkle with toasted sesame seeds.

4. Remember, these are best when served fresh!

07

Tabletop

ANCHORS AWEIGH! LUNCH BAG

SEA GLASS BUCKET CANDLES

BATIK DENIM BEACH BLANKET

Menu

CITRUS SHRIMP

PEPPER-BREAD SALAD WITH
BALSAMIC VINAIGRETTE

CORN FRITTERS

SPICY CHICKEN WINGS

MUFFIN TIN COOKIES X 2

july
BEACH PICNIC

july
BEACH PICNIC

What would a visit to the beach be without refreshments? Whether you are alone or enjoying the day with friends and family, packing up a celebratory picnic makes an incredible day at the beach all the more remarkable. While you are taking in the gifts of the sea, like the soothing colors, the sand between your toes, and the delightful scenery on the shore, you should indulge in all of the gifts that come from the sea as well. So sink your teeth into the following seviche recipe, accompanied by a hearty salad and an over-the-top batch of cookies. Add a casual denim blanket, beach bucket candles, and an adorable tote decorated with sea images, and you have yourself a fantastic celebration at the beach. Even if you cannot get to a shore, you can catch a whiff of the freedom and peace that the ocean brings just by creating some of these recipes and projects.

ANCHORS AWEIGH! LUNCH BAG

I have never been able to dispose of a button. My collection is filled with all different shapes, textures, and colors. Here is a unique way to show off your own button collection and personalize a simple straw bag.

Materials

LARGE WOVEN BEACH BAG IN
A NEUTRAL COLOR

BLUE BUTTONS, ASSORTMENT OF
SIZES AND SHADES

Tools

GLUE GUN

· Lay out the pattern you want to create on your beach bag with the buttons. If you want to stick to a nautical theme, try an anchor, a fish, or a star.

· Using a glue gun, attach the buttons to your bag.

· Fill the bag with your lunch and head to the beach!

SEA GLASS BUCKET CANDLES

This project can be adapted for any theme, indoors or outdoors, simply by changing your colors and design. Visit www.redhillgeneralstore.com to purchase the white buckets.

Materials

ASSORTMENT OF BLUE AND
WHITE SEA GLASS

SMALL WHITE BUCKETS

SAND

TEA LIGHT CANDLES

Tools

GLASS GLUE

· For each bucket, lay out sea glass on a flat surface in a simple nautical pattern.

· Transfer this pattern onto the bucket by attaching the sea glass using glass glue.

· Fill the bucket with sand and place tea lights in the center.

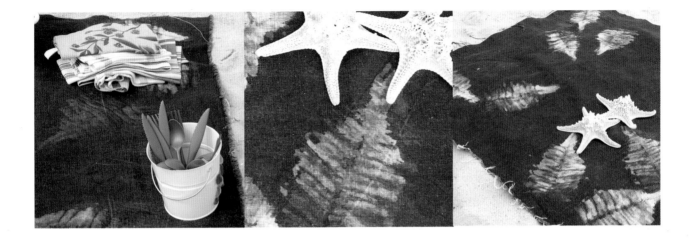

BATIK DENIM BEACH BLANKET

Quite simply one of my favorite projects! If you prefer a different fabric, feel free to mix it up. Try linen or a lightweight fabric—they will absorb the bleach much faster. Also, wider fern leaves will produce a bolder, more graphic pattern. Note that this process is similar to using a bleach pen, in the sense that it will not bleed and you can launder the blanket normally.

Materials

LARGE SQUARE OF DENIM (ABOUT 50 X 50 INCHES)

THICK LIQUID "PREMIUM" BLEACH

ASSORTMENT OF ARTIFICIAL FERN FRONDS

Tools

SANDPAPER

RUBBER GLOVES

CAKE PAN

· Cut a large square of denim as your beach blanket; we chose 50 x 50 inches.

· Sand the areas of the denim where you want to place the fern pattern, and launder the denim.

· Pour the bleach into a cake pan or similar container. Be sure to use rubber gloves when handling the bleach.

· Carefully dip a fern frond into the bleach and "stamp" it onto the denim. To ensure that all the leaves are evenly stamped onto the blanket, quickly run your gloved finger along each frond, pressing it down as you go. Remove the frond. Repeat with the other fronds as desired, creating any pattern you wish.

· Let the bleach set in the denim overnight and launder before using.

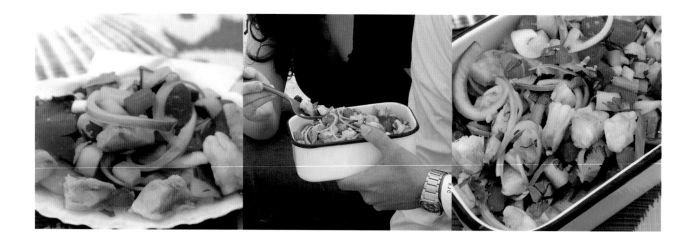

CITRUS SHRIMP

Serves 12

The thing I love about this dish is that you can graze on it all day. That, to me, is the perfect way to enjoy a picnic. And I should tell you that this mixture gets better with time as the flavors marry.

10 CUPS WATER

4 POUNDS SHRIMP, PEELED, TAILS REMOVED

2 CUPS ORANGE JUICE

1¼ CUPS LIME JUICE

¾ CUP OLIVE OIL

8 CLOVES GARLIC, MINCED

2 CUPS FRESH CILANTRO LEAVES, PLUS 4 TABLESPOONS (FOR GARNISH)

1 CUP DICED WATERMELON

1 CUCUMBER, SEEDS REMOVED AND DICED

1 RED ONION, THINLY SLICED

2 TABLESPOONS LEMON JUICE

4 TEASPOONS SALT

1 TEASPOON COARSE BLACK PEPPER

1. In a large pot, bring water to a boil. Add shrimp to boiling water and turn off heat. Let sit 3 minutes. Drain shrimp and rinse in cold water.

2. Coarsely chop shrimp and place in a large bowl. Add orange juice, 1 cup of the lime juice, olive oil, and garlic. Mix well. Place cilantro leaves on top of mixture, cover, and refrigerate overnight.

3. When ready to serve, drain shrimp, reserving ¼ cup of the liquid, and remove cilantro leaves. Add watermelon, cucumber, red onion, lemon juice, the remaining lime juice, the reserved liquid, salt, and pepper. Mix well. Coarsely chop the remaining cilantro and toss into salad.

PEPPER-BREAD SALAD WITH BALSAMIC VINAIGRETTE

Serves 12

This recipe combines two of my all-time favorite things: a delicious baguette with a freshly chopped salad. It's healthy, it's Mediterranean, and it's easy.

Salad

1	BAGUETTE, CUT INTO CUBES
3	TABLESPOONS OLIVE OIL
2	RED BELL PEPPERS
2	GREEN BELL PEPPERS
1	RED ONION

Vinaigrette

¼	CUP BALSAMIC VINEGAR
2	CLOVES GARLIC, FINELY CHOPPED
1	TEASPOON SALT
1	TEASPOON PEPPER
¾	CUP OLIVE OIL

1. For the salad: preheat oven to 375 degrees.

2. Place baguette cubes in a single layer on a baking sheet and drizzle with olive oil. Bake until golden brown and crunchy, about 20 minutes.

3. Thinly slice peppers and onion in a food processor and toss with toasted bread cubes in a large bowl.

4. For the vinaigrette: in a large bowl, mix balsamic vinegar, garlic, salt, and pepper. Whisk in olive oil in a slow, steady stream until all is combined.

5. Pour half of the vinaigrette over the salad and toss. Let sit 5–10 minutes before serving. Serve remaining vinaigrette on the side.

CORN FRITTERS

Serves 12

By starting with Jiffy corn bread mix, you will not believe how easy these flavor-packed fritters are to prepare and enjoy.

2   (8½-OUNCE) PACKAGES
     JIFFY CORN BREAD MIX

2   EGGS

1   CUP MILK

½   TEASPOON CAYENNE PEPPER

½   TEASPOON BLACK PEPPER

2   JALAPEÑO PEPPERS,
     SEEDS REMOVED, CHOPPED

2   CUPS FROZEN SWEET CORN, THAWED

6   GREEN ONIONS, CHOPPED

4   CLOVES GARLIC, CHOPPED

⅔   CUP VEGETABLE OIL

1. Combine all ingredients except for oil and mix well.

2. Add oil to a large skillet and set over medium heat. Once oil is hot, pour 2–3 tablespoons of the corn mixture into the skillet, similar to making a pancake. Repeat with the remaining batter. Cook fritters on one side until lightly browned, then flip over and continue to cook until done.

3. Place fritters on paper towels to cool.

SPICY CHICKEN WINGS

Serves 12

Simply finger-lickin' good.

1   CUP SOY SAUCE

½   CUP VEGETABLE OIL

2   PACKETS FAJITA OR TACO SEASONING

4   POUNDS CHICKEN WINGS

1. Preheat oven to 375 degrees.

2. In a large zip-locking plastic bag, combine soy sauce, oil, and fajita seasoning. Add chicken wings to marinade and let sit in refrigerator at least 4 hours or overnight.

3. Place wings on a baking sheet covered with aluminum foil and bake for 30–35 minutes.

MUFFIN TIN COOKIES X 2

Serves 12 (makes 24)

I just love when a recipe can go a couple different ways—it's like two for the price of one. In this case, it is half the amount of work for twice the goodness. Make one, get one free!

Cookie Base

2½ CUPS FLOUR

1 TEASPOON COARSE SALT

1½ STICKS UNSALTED BUTTER, SOFTENED

1 CUP SUGAR

1 EGG

1 TEASPOON VANILLA

¼ CUP WATER (OPTIONAL)

1. Preheat oven to 350 degrees.

2. In a medium bowl, mix together flour and salt. Set aside. Beat butter and sugar together until creamy and fluffy. Add egg and vanilla, and continue to beat until smooth. Add flour mixture and mix until just combined. If dough seems too dry, add water. Divide dough in half.

Caramel Chocolate version

6 OUNCES BAKER'S SEMISWEET CHOCOLATE, CHOPPED

1 TABLESPOON VEGETABLE OIL

12 CARAMEL-FILLED HERSHEY'S KISSES

1. In a small saucepan, melt chocolate squares and vegetable oil together. Once melted, fold into one half of the cookie dough base until combined. Roll dough into a 12-inch log and wrap in plastic. Let rest in freezer 10 minutes.

2. Once rested, slice the dough log into 1-inch rounds. Lay rounds flat in muffin tins fitted with paper or foil baking cups, and stick a Hershey's Kiss upside down in each.

3. Bake 20–25 minutes.

Sweet and Salty version

1 TEASPOON LEMON JUICE

2 TEASPOONS DECORATING SUGAR

½ CUP COARSELY CHOPPED SALTED PRETZELS

1. Fold lemon juice into remaining half of dough. Roll dough into a 12-inch log and wrap in plastic. Let rest in freezer 10 minutes.

2. Once rested, slice the dough log into 1-inch rounds. Lay rounds flat in muffin tins fitted with paper or foil baking cups, and sprinkle each with ½ teaspoon decorating sugar and 1 teaspoon of the crushed pretzel.

3. Bake 20–25 minutes.

08

august
FAMILY COOKOUT

august
FAMILY COOKOUT

Every year it happens, and every year might even be more fun than the last. I am talking, of course, about my family picnic. Come summertime, the annual party planning dilemmas among my sisters and me ensue. Will the food be served family-style or buffet? Will we serve all hot food or some cold? How many tables and chairs will we need? But when the day finally comes and the guests arrive at our lakeside cottage, none of it matters, because once again we are all together: my uncle who stitched up my head when it got cut in a game of chicken, my cousin who first introduced me to Bruce Spring-steen, and my aunt who taught me Sunday school for what seemed like my entire childhood. My faithful crew of family attended my games, listened patiently to my stories, and always inspired me when I needed it. I was dealt a lucky hand when God was passing out family, and the best way I know to honor them is to gather them so we can all feel the love that only togetherness can bring.

FRUIT OR VEGGIE CENTERPIECES

I warn you: this is time-consuming; but trust me—it will be so stunning.

Materials

BRIGHT, IN-SEASON VEGETABLES
OR FRUITS

ASSORTED STYROFOAM CONES

Tools

TOOTHPICKS

- At your local farmstand, pick the freshest and most color-ful vegetables or fruits. We chose asparagus, radishes, and brussels sprouts.

- Place a toothpick in the back of the individual vegetables/fruits.

- Arrange the vegetables/fruits on the Styrofoam cones to create beautiful, fresh, and colorful centerpieces! Use the leaves of the vegetables, or any other live greenery you may have, to cover the surfaces as well.

- To avoid wilting and to get the best look, make the centerpieces the day of the event, or wrap them in plastic and store them in the refrigerator.

ETCHED KEEPSAKE BOXES

This project requires a special tool; however, beware, because when you buy it, you will be running around looking for new things to brand.

Materials

SMALL WOODEN BOXES

FAMILY KEEPSAKES SUCH AS
PHOTOS, DRIED FERNS AND OTHER
FLORA, A FAVORITE FAMILY DESSERT
OR CANDY, A FAMILY CHARM,
ETC.

GREEN RAFFIA

- For each box, attach the letter or pattern of your choice to the branding tool. Preheat.

- Press the branding tool into the corner of the lid of the box, evenly distributing pressure. Remove quickly.

- Fill the box with family keepsakes.

- Tie up the boxes with raffia and give one away to each guest.

Tools

WALNUT HOLLOW WOODBURNER
(BRANDING) TOOL WITH LETTER
ATTACHMENTS

FLATWARE FOLD-UPS

If you have old, stained cloth napkins, use them for this project and simply hide any unsightly sections with a patch. Who said patches were just for pants?

Materials

CLOTH NAPKINS

IRON-ON PATCHES

Tools

IRON

SCISSORS

- Buy colorful, inexpensive napkins and fold them as you would to set a table.

- Trim your patches to fit on the folded napkins, leaving plenty of room for your silverware to fit inside them.

- Iron along three sides of each patch to seal it onto each napkin. Place your silverware inside the pockets.

GRILLED PORK RIBS

Serves 20 (makes 3 whole sparerib racks)

Ribs are my husband's absolute favorite things, and this recipe . . . well, let's just say if I make it for him, the sky is the limit.

¾ TEASPOON GARLIC POWDER

⅜ TEASPOON GROUND CELERY SEED

6 TEASPOONS SMOKED PAPRIKA

9 TABLESPOONS LIGHT BROWN SUGAR

1½ TEASPOONS CUMIN

1½ TEASPOONS CAYENNE PEPPER

3 TABLESPOONS SALT

1½ TEASPOONS BLACK PEPPER

3 PORK SPARERIB RACKS

1. Mix all dry ingredients in a bowl, and with your hands rub each sparerib rack generously with spice mixture.

2. Stack sparerib racks on top of one another and wrap in plastic. Refrigerate overnight.

3. Preheat grill to medium. Remove ribs from wrap and place on top rack of grill. Reduce heat to low, cook for 45 minutes, flip, and cook for another 45 minutes.

BEEF BRISKET

Serves 20 (makes 2 briskets)

Yes, this is the second meat recipe on this menu; when you're from a big Midwestern family, it's not a reunion without the meat! Moreover, since this brisket is prepared in the oven, you can have it cooking while the pork ribs are on the grill.

Dry Rub

1	CUP BROWN SUGAR
4	TABLESPOONS SALT
2	TEASPOONS SMOKED PAPRIKA
½	TEASPOON CINNAMON
2	TEASPOONS BLACK PEPPER
4	TABLESPOONS THYME

Brisket

2	LARGE BEEF BRISKETS, TRIMMED
	OLIVE OIL
2	LARGE LEEKS, CUT IN HALF AND SLICED
2	LARGE RED ONIONS, SLICED
2	LARGE ONIONS, SLICED
8	CLOVES GARLIC, SMASHED
2	BAY LEAVES
2	(28-OUNCE) CANS CRUSHED TOMATOES
⅔	CUP BALSAMIC VINEGAR
2–4	CUPS CHICKEN STOCK

1. Preheat oven to 350 degrees.

2. Mix all dry-rub ingredients together and rub over entire briskets with hands. Wrap briskets in plastic and refrigerate overnight.

3. Heat a large roasting pan on medium-high. Remove briskets from plastic. When pan is hot, add olive oil, and when pan is smoking hot, sear beef on each side for 5 minutes, to achieve a nice golden crust.

4. Remove briskets from pan and add leeks, onions, garlic, and bay leaves. Cook until translucent. Add crushed tomatoes, vinegar, and stock. Place briskets on top of onions and cover pan tightly with aluminum foil. Place pan in oven and cook for 2½ hours, turning briskets over halfway through the cooking process.

THREE-BEAN SALAD

Serves 20

To properly blanch vegetables, place them in very salty boiling water. Remove the vegetables as soon as they are cooked and cool them under cold water or, even better, in a bowl of ice water. This process helps preserve the vegetables' vibrant color.

Vinaigrette

- ½ CUP CHOPPED FRESH TARRAGON
- ½ CUP CHOPPED FRESH CHERVIL
- 3 TABLESPOONS RED WINE VINEGAR
- 2 TABLESPOONS BALSAMIC VINEGAR
- 1 TABLESPOON HONEY
- ⅓ CUP EXTRA-VIRGIN OLIVE OIL

Salad

- 4 QUARTS WATER
- ½ CUP SALT
- 6 CUPS STRING BEANS, CUT IN HALF
- 6 CUPS YELLOW WAX BEANS, CUT IN HALF
- 3 (15½-OUNCE) CANS CANNELLINI BEANS
- 3 CUPS THINLY SLICED RED ONION
- SALT AND PEPPER TO TASTE

1. For the vinaigrette: in a large mixing bowl, combine tarragon, chervil, vinegars, honey, and olive oil.

2. For the salad: bring water to a boil; add salt and green and yellow beans. Cook until tender but still a little crisp, about 6 minutes. Cool under cold water or in ice bath.

3. Rinse cannellini beans thoroughly. Add cannellini, onion, and green and yellow beans to vinaigrette. Add salt and pepper to taste and mix well.

4. Let salad marinate for at least 2 hours in refrigerator before serving.

WHOLE-GRAIN POTATO SALAD

Serves 20

This is one of my favorite ways to prepare potato salad. The bite and texture added by the mustard are just right.

40 BABY RED POTATOES

40 BABY YUKON GOLD POTATOES

⅓ CUP SALT

3 TABLESPOONS CARAWAY SEEDS

2 CUPS SOUR CREAM

1 CUP MAYONNAISE

¼ CUP WHITE WINE VINEGAR

1 CUP WHOLE-GRAIN DIJON MUSTARD

1 CUP CHOPPED FRESH CHIVES

SALT AND BLACK PEPPER TO TASTE

1. Place potatoes in two large pots, cover with water, and distribute salt equally between the two pots. Cover and bring to a simmer. Cook until potatoes are tender. Check by inserting a knife or toothpick; if there is no resistance, the potatoes are done. Always check the largest potato, as it takes the longest to cook.

2. Allow potatoes to cool, and cut them into quarters.

3. Toast caraway seeds for 5 minutes in a small pan over medium heat, and put into a large mixing bowl. Add sour cream, mayonnaise, vinegar, mustard, and chives, and whisk to combine. Add potatoes and mix well to coat evenly. Season to taste with salt and pepper.

PEANUT BRITTLE

Serves 20

This is one of my favorite treats Grandmother, aka "Mom Brown," used to make. I can hardly taste it without smelling her kitchen! Be sure to have a candy thermometer on hand for this one.

COOKING OIL OR NONSTICK COOKING SPRAY

6 CUPS SUGAR

3 CUPS LIGHT CORN SYRUP

2¼ CUPS WATER

6 CUPS DRY-ROASTED UNSALTED PEANUTS

2½ TEASPOONS SALT

6 TABLESPOONS UNSALTED BUTTER

2 TABLESPOONS BAKING SODA

1. Grease 2 large baking sheets with oil or nonstick spray.

2. In a large saucepan, combine sugar, corn syrup, and water. Place on high heat, stirring until the sugar dissolves.

3. When the candy thermometer registers 250 degrees, the softball stage, add peanuts and salt. Continue to cook, stirring often.

4. When thermometer reads 290 degrees, remove pan from heat.

5. Add butter and baking soda to hot sugar and stir to combine. Pour hot mixture onto prepared baking sheets and spread evenly to desired thickness with a spatula.

6. Allow candy to sit until it hardens. Break up with your fingers.

APPLE BROWNIES

Serves 20 (makes two 13 x 9-inch pans)

This is a recipe I got from my father-in-law's wife, Gail. I took one look and I knew I had to serve it up in my next book. So here you go: it's simple, quick, and yummy. Thanks, Gail!

6   EGGS

3½ CUPS SUGAR

2   CUPS VEGETABLE OIL

2   TEASPOONS VANILLA

4   CUPS ALL-PURPOSE FLOUR

2   TEASPOONS CINNAMON

2   TEASPOONS BAKING POWDER

1   TEASPOON SALT

4   CUPS DICED APPLES

     NONSTICK COOKING SPRAY

1. Preheat oven to 350 degrees.

2. In a large mixing bowl, beat eggs and sugar until fluffy and pale. Add oil and vanilla; mix well. Sift dry ingredients and mix into the egg mixture. Stir in apples.

3. Coat two 13 x 9-inch pans with nonstick spray and spread batter evenly into pans. Bake until a toothpick inserted into the center comes out clean, 45–50 minutes.

09

Tabletop
MONKEYING AROUND

SUITCASE FAVORS

PAINT-BY-LEAF CANVAS

Menu
ZEBRA MAC 'N' CHEESE

POTATO CHIP CHICKEN FINGER
ROLL-UPS WITH CARROT RIBBONS

VEGGIE STRIP MOUNTAIN

HONEY AND MINT MANGO SALAD

ELEPHANT TRUNKS

INSECT JIGGLERS

september
PLAYFUL SAFARI SPREAD

september
PLAYFUL SAFARI SPREAD

i am sure you have heard the expression "Girls like sugar and spice and everything nice." Growing up in a family with two sisters, and now having a baby girl of my own, I can say with confidence that there is a great amount of truth to that statement. Boys, on the other hand, tend to be quite the opposite. And that is why I have planned a boy's birthday party around nothing sugary, spicy, or nice. Instead I have turned to the great outdoors for a whimsical safari-style, down-and-dirty celebration. I think it is a great idea to anchor your party around some outside structure, whether it be a tepee, a tree house, or a swing set. In this chapter, I'll show you how to create an interactive throw that can serve as a backdrop and a picnic blanket for your warriors. This safari is complete with masks, monkeys, and food reminiscent of all things wild—zucchini mountains, elephant trunk chocolate-dipped bananas, and rugged chicken wraps, followed by zebra-striped mac 'n' cheese. So flip these next pages and start daydreaming about your own walk on the wild side, designed specifically for the adventurous boy in all of us.

MONKEYING AROUND

This is a project that Kyle on my team created, and it is a favorite at the Katie Brown Workshop. You can find these cardboard plaques at your local craft store. Feel free to get creative and see what else the craft store has in stock—anything cardboard-based will work; you can even use plain cardboard that you cut to shape. We suggest beading some leather rope to hang in between the monkeys for a bit of variety.

Materials

HANGING CARDBOARD PLAQUES (CIRCLES, RECTANGLES, AND OVALS)

TAN CONSTRUCTION PAPER

THICK POPSICLE / CRAFT STICKS

ASSORTED BUTTONS (BLACK, RED, ORANGE, BROWN)

RUBBER CEMENT

ROPE

BARK-COVERED WIRE

Tools

LARGE OVAL-SHAPED PAPER PUNCH

GLUE GUN

X-ACTO KNIFE

SCISSORS

- For each monkey, pick a plaque to use as the head. Using the paper punch, cut an oval mouth from the construction paper and attach with rubber cement. Next, make the eyes and mouth: cut off the rounded ends of a craft stick and use them for eyes; make the mouth with the remaining middle portion of the craft stick. Add buttons for pupils and nostrils. Attach them all with hot glue.

- Pick a second plaque to use as the body of the monkey. Using an X-Acto knife, cut a large hole in the bottom of the head plaque, and slide it over the body plaque. Secure the pieces with hot glue where necessary.

- Cut the rope to various lengths for the ears, legs, and arms. To give the arms and legs extra support, wrap bark-covered wire around the rope. This gives the monkeys a bit more stability, which will allow them to hang from one another.

- To attach the arms, legs, and ears to the monkey, you will need to cut holes into the cardboard plaques in the appropriate places.

- Insert the rope for the arms, legs, and ears into the holes you've made, securing them with hot glue.

- Hang the monkeys from one another to create the perfect jungle scene!

SUITCASE FAVORS

This project is a great use of old belts and plain cardboard boxes. If you're using a woven belt, as we have, dab a little hot glue under the ends to keep them from unraveling.

Materials

BROWN CARDBOARD BOXES,
APPROXIMATELY 11 X 8 X 5 INCHES

OLD WOVEN BELTS

BRADS (4 FOR EACH SUITCASE)

BLACK INK PAD

GIVEAWAY GIFTS

Tools

AWL

"WORLD" STAMP SET

SCISSORS

- For each suitcase, using an awl, punch 4 holes into the top of the box for the handle. Cut a woven belt to size for the handle. Place 2 brads through one end of the belt and through the holes in the box, and fold the brads under the box to hold them in place. Repeat on the opposite side of the belt.

- Stamp the pattern of your choice onto the box to give it that perfect worn-in and well-traveled feel, like a box that's been around the world or the passport of a world traveler.

- Fill each box with the giveaways of your choice.

PAINT-BY-LEAF CANVAS

This is a project that will get all the kids involved! It is a real "Our Gang" kind of backdrop for a safari party, especially if you do not have a rain forest in your backyard.

Materials

CANVAS ON A ROLL

LARGE ARTIFICIAL JUNGLE LEAVES AND FRONDS

ASSORTED GREEN AND BROWN TEMPERA PAINTS

Tools

PENCIL

BLACK MARKER

ASSORTED SPONGE PAINTBRUSHES

- Unroll the canvas and lay out the artificial leaves to create a jungle scene.

- Carefully trace around the leaves with a pencil onto the canvas.

- Go over the pencil with a black marker, adding each child's name at his or her place setting.

- Place paints and brushes on the canvas and let the kids create their own jungle scene!

ZEBRA MAC 'N' CHEESE

Serves 10

I know everyone thinks they have the best mac 'n' cheese recipe, and let's be honest, it is tough to beat the blue-box variety. But I promise: the following recipe is really the best.

2 TABLESPOONS BUTTER

2 TABLESPOONS FLOUR

1 CUP MILK

1 CUP CHICKEN BROTH

½ CUP CREAM CHEESE

5 CUPS GRATED SHARP YELLOW CHEDDAR CHEESE

1 POUND ELBOW PASTA, COOKED IN EQUAL PARTS CHICKEN STOCK AND WATER

   SALT AND PEPPER TO TASTE

1 CUP GRATED SHARP WHITE CHEDDAR CHEESE

1. In a large saucepan, melt butter on medium heat. Once melted, add flour and cook for about 2 minutes (this is a roux). Slowly whisk in milk and chicken broth. When milk begins to steam, whisk in cream cheese until smooth.

2. Turn off the heat and add 4 cups of the yellow cheddar, stirring until melted and smooth. Pour the sauce over the pasta and stir until thoroughly mixed. Add salt and pepper to taste.

3. Put the macaroni into individual ramekins or fry pans. Top each ramekin with the remaining yellow and the white grated cheese, alternating each to create a striped "zebra" pattern. Place the ramekins under a broiler or in a warm oven until cheese is just melted. (Don't let them heat too long, or the cheese toppings will run together.)

POTATO CHIP CHICKEN FINGER ROLL-UPS
WITH CARROT RIBBONS

Serves 10

If your kids are adventurous eaters, change up the sauce in these roll-ups and see what they think. Honey mustard is a favorite of mine, as well as hummus or salsa.

Chicken Fingers

20 CHICKEN TENDERS

1   CUP FLOUR

3   EGGS

⅓ CUP MILK

1   (14-OUNCE) BAG POTATO CHIPS

Roll-Ups

10 FLOUR TORTILLAS

1   CARROT, PEELED

10 LEAVES BOSTON LETTUCE (OR
    SIMILAR GREEN WITH SOFT
    LEAVES)

1   CUP RANCH DRESSING

1. For the chicken fingers: preheat oven to 350 degrees.

2. Set up an assembly line for the chicken tenders. First, fill a medium-size bowl with flour. In a second bowl, whisk eggs and milk together and set it beside flour bowl. Slightly open bag of chips (to let the air out) and crush them until they are in small pieces. Place bag of crushed chips at the end of your assembly line.

3. Dredge 1 chicken finger through flour and shake off excess. Next, coat it in egg mixture, then drop it into chip bag. Repeat with the rest of the chicken tenders. Once all tenders are in chip bag, shake them around until they are all fully coated with potato chip flakes. Place tenders in a single layer on a baking sheet and bake for 25 minutes.

4. For the roll-ups: while chicken fingers are baking, prepare the tortillas. Place tortillas between wet paper towels on a baking sheet and put sheet in the oven. This will make the tortillas softer and easier to fold.

5. Meanwhile, using a vegetable peeler, peel long, thin strips off the sides of the carrot. Remove tortillas from oven and place a few ribbons of carrot in each tortilla, in addition to a leaf of lettuce and about 1 tablespoon of the ranch dressing.

6. Remove chicken fingers from oven. When they have cooled slightly, add 2 strips to each tortilla and wrap tightly.

VEGGIE STRIP MOUNTAIN

Serves 10

Doesn't every jungle have a mountain?

6 CUPS VEGETABLE OIL

6 ZUCCHINIS, PEELED

8 SQUASHES, PEELED

½ CUP FLOUR

   SALT TO TASTE

1. Heat oil in a large, heavy pot over high heat.

2. Using a potato peeler, peel long strips from zucchinis and squashes. They should look like thin ribbons. When you reach the seedy center, set aside. Put strips into a large bowl and toss with flour, making sure each strip is coated.

3. Separate strips into small batches and fry until golden brown, about 7–10 minutes (you will know the oil is ready when a small pinch of flour dropped into it sizzles immediately). After removing strips from oil, spread them on paper towels to drain, and sprinkle with salt. Arrange strips into a mound and serve immediately.

HONEY AND MINT MANGO SALAD

Serves 10

Chiffonade is the term used when cutting herbs into ribbons. The technique is simple, the result elegant. Just tightly roll the leaves (like rolling a cigar) and cut them crosswise into thin strips. I love the sweet honey mixed with strings of fresh mint and tossed with juicy bites of mango in this salad.

Glaze

½ CUP HONEY

2 TABLESPOONS FRESH MINT, CUT INTO RIBBONS

Salad

2 MANGOES, CUT INTO SMALL CHUNKS

2 PINEAPPLES, CUT INTO SMALL CHUNKS

¼ TEASPOON POPPY SEEDS

1. For the glaze: pour honey into a medium saucepan and set over low heat. Melt honey until it is easily poured, about 2 minutes. Add 1 tablespoon of the mint leaves to the honey and let sit 2–3 minutes.

2. For the salad: in a large bowl, combine mangoes and pineapples. Pour glaze over fruit and toss. Sprinkle with the remaining mint and the poppy seeds.

ELEPHANT TRUNKS

Serves 10

What kid doesn't love chocolate? Be sure to mix in a little vegetable oil to keep the melted chocolate from getting overheated and clumpy.

10 POPSICLE STICKS

5 BANANAS, CUT IN HALF

2 TABLESPOONS VEGETABLE OIL

24 OUNCES SEMISWEET BAKER'S CHOCOLATE, CHOPPED

TOPPINGS: PEANUTS, COCONUT, OR CRUSHED NILLA WAFERS

1. Stick Popsicle sticks into cut ends of bananas and place on a baking sheet fitted with wax paper. Place sheet in the freezer.

2. Fill a medium-size pot with approximately 2 inches of water and place on the stove on high heat. When water boils, turn heat to low and nest a glass bowl in the top of the pot. Make sure bottom of bowl is not touching water. Add oil and chocolate to bowl and melt, stirring often.

3. Once chocolate has melted, remove bananas from freezer. One by one, dip bananas in chocolate and coat completely. Hold coated bananas above chocolate for a few seconds to allow excess chocolate to drip off.

4. Once a banana is coated with chocolate, hold it above the topping bowl and sprinkle all sides of banana with topping before returning it to wax paper.

5. Place bananas in the refrigerator to set, about 10 minutes.

INSECT JIGGLERS

Serves 10–12 (makes 24)

This is a great way to incorporate a fun touch of the wild. Your mini-guests will giggle while enjoying these jigglers.

A VARIETY OF INSECT-SHAPED GUMMY CANDIES

4 (4-SERVING-SIZE) PACKAGES JELL-O FLAVORED GELATIN

2½ CUPS BOILING WATER

1. Place an insect candy in the center of each silicone mold or minimuffin tin.

2. Mix gelatin with boiling water and stir until dissolved, about 3 minutes. Set aside and let cool for about 5 minutes.

3. Fill each mold with gelatin and place in refrigerator until set, about 2 hours.

Tabletop

HANGING LANTERNS

BRANCHING OUT

SILVERWARE ENVELOPES

Menu

MAKE-YOUR-OWN SANDWICH BAR

Herbed Flatbread

Grilled Hanger Steak

Grilled Side of Salmon

Chimichurri Sauce

Horseradish Crème

Spicy Red Pepper Relish

Caramelized Pearl Onions

HERBED PASTA SALAD
WITH GARLIC AIOLI CREAM

PASSION FRUIT CRÈME POTS

october
ENGAGEMENT BUFFET

ENGAGEMENT BUFFET

i just threw my first-ever engagement party. It was for one of my best friends, and although I had heard it rumored that every bride turns into a bridezilla, I was pretty sure that was not going to happen to my friend. She could not nor would she ever be a bridezilla . . . or so I thought. I should have realized I was in trouble when she gave me a list of 115 people she intended to invite. Because I was the host, I assumed that I would be allowed to choose the location. Not so. She mentioned a few places, which I dutifully called, the first of which cost $100,000. I could hear the disappointment on the other end of the phone as I relayed the news to my friend. After great reluctance, she finally agreed to an out-of-the-way bar I suggested. It was then that I began to suspect that I had an emerging bridezilla on my hands. Bad went to worse as I was greeted with silence after describing my genius ideas for tabletop decorations, themes, and decor. I then realized that I was dealing with a full-blown demanding diva.

However, the night of the party, as the music pulsed and the champagne flowed, the old familiar friend I knew and loved reemerged. She was thrilled with each toast and song presented in her honor. The centerpieces soon became perfect in her eyes, and the relaxed mood set by the restaurant only fueled everybody's sense of love and celebration. So indulge the bridezillas in your life with a once-in-a-lifetime fete—just remember to bring your patience along with the roses.

HANGING LANTERNS

BRANCHING OUT

You can create such interesting tablescapes by taking things that normally don't go on the dinner table and placing them there— they're surprising and make for good conversation pieces. And the thing about using lanterns is that there is usually a way to weave a bit of your design and color scheme into the hardware of the lamp.

Who says you can use only flowers to create beautiful bouquets?

Materials

BLACK HANGING LANTERNS

ASSORTED PINK AND WHITE RIBBONS, VARIOUS WIDTHS

PILLAR CANDLES

Tools

SCISSORS

GLUE GUN

- Remove the glass panes from the lanterns.
- Weave the ribbon on the inside of the metal shell of each lantern, using hot glue to attach the ribbon where necessary. Use a nice variety of thick and thin, graphic and plain ribbons.
- Replace the glass panes in the lanterns. (This ensures that the ribbon will not be exposed to the flame.)
- Hang the lanterns from various heights and place some on the tabletop. Set pillar candles inside the lanterns and light.

Materials

ASSORTED TWIGS

LARGE VASES

Tools

WHITE SPRAY PAINT

PINK SPRAY PAINT

- Gather a bundle of tall twigs from your local floral supply store.
- In order to get the most vibrant color on these dark sticks, prime them with a coat of white spray paint first.
- Coat the twigs with the pink spray paint, place them in large vases, and arrange the vases on the tabletop.

SILVERWARE ENVELOPES

If you want to add a little more pizzazz to these roll-ups, hand-stitch the sides with a large needle and colorful embroidery thread.

Materials

BLACK VINYL FABRIC

WIDE PINK RIBBON

SILVER BRADS

Tools

SCISSORS

PLASTIC/WATERPROOF GLUE

HOLE PUNCH

· For each envelope, cut the fabric in a long rectangular shape, about three times the length that you'll want your finished envelope. (Since you're using vinyl, you don't have to worry about the edges fraying.)

· Fold up the bottom of the fabric, creating a pocket for the silverware. Ensure that you have enough room for the silverware to fit inside the pocket. Seal the edges of the pocket with plastic glue.

· Attach the ribbon to the center of the inside of the flap using plastic glue. To do this, tuck and glue the end of the ribbon inside the top of the pocket and continue running the ribbon up the inside of the flap, tacking with glue in spots.

· Flip the top over and tuck the unfinished edge under to create a finished seam. Hold the loop in place and pin it down with a silver brad (create the hole for the brad with a hole punch), going through the fabric and top layers of ribbon.

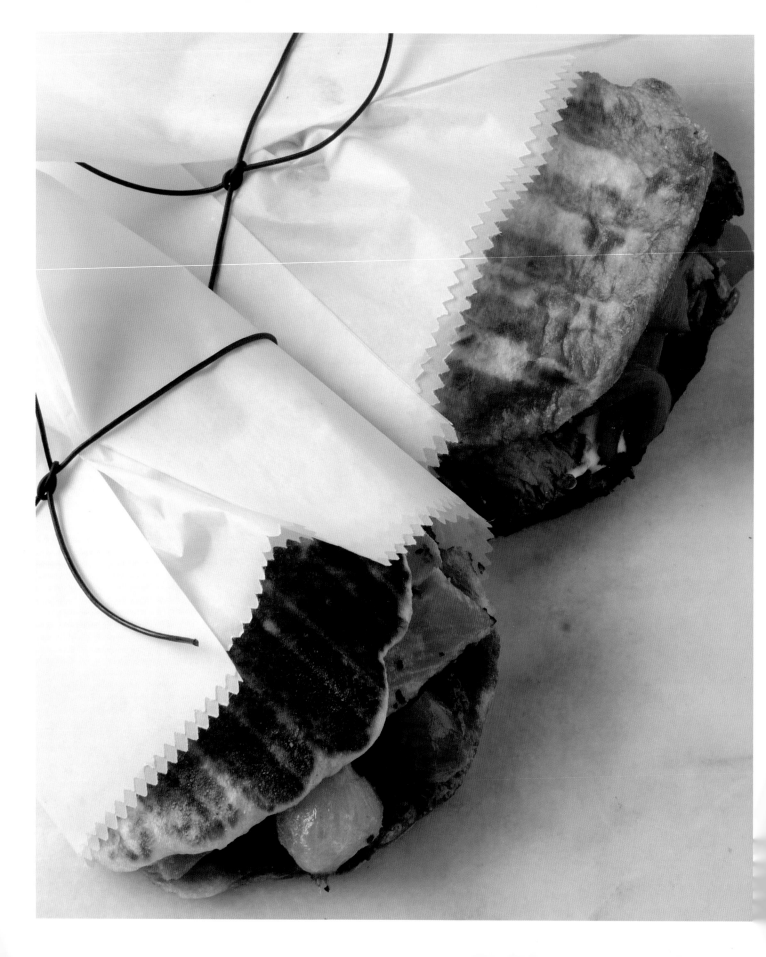

Make-Your-Own Sandwich Bar

HERBED FLATBREAD

Makes 16

This is a great way to bring the flavor and feel of homemade bread to your tabletop in a quarter of the time. You may want to suggest that your guests create an open-faced or a traditional sandwich, in which case you should double the recipe. Feel free to mix and match the following meats and sauces to create uniquely delicious flatbread sandwiches!

2 POUNDS FROZEN
   PIZZA DOUGH

   FLOUR FOR DUSTING

2 EGG WHITES

16 FRESH BASIL LEAVES
   (OR OTHER FRESH HERB OF YOUR CHOICE)

2 TABLESPOONS OLIVE OIL

1. Divide dough into 16 balls, dust your surface with flour, and roll out each ball to about ½-inch thickness.

2. With a pastry brush, place a dollop of egg white in the center of each flatbread and "paste" on a basil leaf.

3. Heat a ridged griddle or skillet over medium-high heat and add olive oil.

4. Place flatbreads basil side down on griddle and let cook until browned, about 2 minutes. Flip and repeat. Add more olive oil if needed.

5. Let flatbreads cool on wire racks.

Make-Your-Own Sandwich Bar

GRILLED HANGER STEAK

Serves 16

Hanger steak is highly underrated. Cook and you shall see!

3–4 POUND HANGER STEAK

4 TABLESPOONS OLIVE OIL

3 TEASPOONS COARSE SALT

2 TEASPOONS COARSE BLACK PEPPER

1. Preheat grill to 400–450 degrees.

2. Drizzle steak with oil and season with salt and pepper.

3. Place steak on heated grill for about 5–7 minutes per side for medium to medium-rare. Let sit, covered, for 5–10 minutes before serving.

GRILLED SIDE OF SALMON

Serves 16

There's nothing fishy about how delicious this recipe is!

3–4 POUND SALMON SIDE, SKIN ATTACHED

2 TABLESPOONS VEGETABLE OIL

1½ TEASPOONS COARSE SALT

1 TEASPOON COARSE BLACK PEPPER

1. Preheat grill to 400–450 degrees.

2. Place salmon, skin side down, on a piece of foil that has been covered with oil. Make sure foil extends 3–4 inches from each side of fish. Sprinkle salt and pepper evenly over top of fish and place fish on the grill, lid closed, for approximately 10 minutes. Carefully remove fish from grill, making sure not to spill oil, and let sit, covered, for 5–10 minutes before serving.

Make-Your-Own Sandwich Bar

CHIMICHURRI SAUCE
Makes approximately 1½ cups

This adds just the right pinch of flavor to many a sandwich. It is paired best with hanger steak.

1   CUP FRESH PARSLEY LEAVES
    (ABOUT 1 BUNCH)
2   SHALLOTS, PEELED
3   GARLIC CLOVES, PEELED
¼   CUP RED WINE VINEGAR
1   TABLESPOON LEMON JUICE
1   CUP OLIVE OIL
1   TEASPOON SALT

1. Put parsley, shallots, and garlic into the bowl of a food processor. Pulse until coarsely chopped.

2. Add vinegar and lemon juice, and pulse 3–4 times.

3. Turn food processor on low and add oil in a slow, steady stream. Store sauce in an airtight container and refrigerate overnight.

HORSERADISH CRÈME
Makes approximately 1½ cups

Don't panic when you see crème fraîche on the ingredient list. You can buy it in the dairy section of just about any grocery store. This crème is paired best with hanger steak.

1   CUP CRÈME FRAÎCHE
4   TABLESPOONS HORSERADISH CREAM
½   TEASPOON SALT
½   TEASPOON PEPPER
¼   TEASPOON SMOKED PAPRIKA

Combine all ingredients and mix thoroughly. Store crème in an airtight container and refrigerate overnight.

CARAMELIZED PEARL ONIONS
Serves 16

Another essential element to any great sandwich bar. These are perfect for the hanger steak or the grilled salmon.

3   (16-OUNCE) BAGS PEARL ONIONS
3   TABLESPOONS BUTTER
3   TEASPOONS SALT
1   TEASPOON SUGAR

1. Peel onions and place in a large saucepan. Add enough water to saucepan to come halfway up sides of onions. Add butter, salt, and sugar, and place saucepan over medium-high heat. Bring the mixture to a boil, then reduce heat to medium and partially cover pan until the liquid reduces and turns into syrup.

2. Once syrup begins to turn a caramel color, add 1–2 tablespoons water and stir onions so they pick up the color. Repeat this step until onions reach desired brownness. Before serving, break up onions with a spoon to make them easier to use as a condiment.

SPICY RED PEPPER RELISH
Serves 16

This relish will add spice to your sandwich ensemble. It is paired best with grilled side of salmon.

2   (16-OUNCE) JARS ROASTED RED PEPPERS, DRAINED
2   (4-OUNCE) CANS DICED JALAPEÑO PEPPERS, DRAINED
    SALT AND PEPPER TO TASTE

Slice red peppers into thin strips and combine in a medium-size bowl with jalapeños. Add salt and pepper to taste.

HERBED PASTA SALAD WITH GARLIC AIOLI CREAM   *Serves 16*

This pasta salad is a happy marriage of mouth-watering flavors.

Pasta Salad

4   ZUCCHINIS

5   SUMMER SQUASHES

⅓   CUP OLIVE OIL

½   TABLESPOON LEMON JUICE

1½ CUPS CUBED THICK-SLICED SMOKED BACON, COOKED UNTIL CRISPY

1½ CUPS COARSELY CHOPPED KALAMATA OLIVES

2   CUPS HALVED CHERRY TOMATOES

2   POUNDS COOKED PENNE PASTA, COOLED

2   TABLESPOONS CHOPPED FRESH PARSLEY

    SALT AND PEPPER TO TASTE

Cream

1   HEAD GARLIC

2   TABLESPOONS OLIVE OIL

2   CUPS CREAM

¼   CUP CHICKEN BROTH

½   CUP MAYONNAISE

½   TEASPOON SALT

1. For the cream: preheat oven to 375 degrees.

2. Slice top off head of garlic, exposing cloves. Place cut side up on a sheet of foil large enough to wrap around entire head of garlic. Pour olive oil over exposed garlic cloves and wrap tightly with foil. Place on a baking sheet and bake until garlic is soft, 25–30 minutes. Cool.

3. In a medium saucepan, combine cream and chicken broth. Bring to a boil, then lower heat and reduce until about 1¼ cups remain, about 20 minutes.

4. For the pasta salad: while cream is reducing, preheat grill to 350–400 degrees. Slice squashes and zucchinis lengthwise in ½-inch slices and drizzle with olive oil. Grill 3–4 minutes per side, turning once. Slightly cool and cut into chunks. In a large bowl, mix squash, zucchini, lemon juice, bacon, olives, and tomatoes. Add pasta and gently toss.

5. Finish cream by squeezing garlic cloves into a medium-size bowl and mixing with mayonnaise. Whisk in cream mixture until smooth. Pour 1 cup of cream over pasta salad, and serve remaining cream on the side. Add parsley and salt and pepper to taste to pasta salad.

PASSION FRUIT CRÈME POTS

Serves 16

This delight will make you pucker—it has such a zing to it!

6 CUPS MELTED PASSION FRUIT
   SORBET

24 EGG YOLKS

8 TABLESPOONS SUGAR

5 CUPS HEAVY CREAM

2 CUPS WHOLE MILK

   FRESH MINT FOR GARNISH

1. Preheat oven to 300 degrees.

2. In a large saucepot, bring sorbet to a boil, then bring down to a simmer and reduce by half. Let cool.

3. In a large bowl, whisk egg yolks and sugar together. Add cream, milk, and reduced sorbet. Stir to combine.

4. Place 16 ramekins in shallow baking dishes filled with water. Water should come halfway up sides of ramekins. Fill each ramekin three-quarters full with passion fruit mixture. Bake until centers of crème pots are set, 35–40 minutes. Refrigerate for at least 2 hours before serving. Garnish with fresh mint.

november
THANKSGIVING SUPPER

This is my holiday. To me it does not get better than Thanksgiving. Sure, it's a lot of work making the guest list, choosing the menu, unpacking the good china, and of course, cooking. But what fun! Because to me Thanksgiving is all about food, and one of my favorite pastimes is cooking, Thanksgiving is more like a labor of love. I spend weeks poring over magazines and looking through cookbooks, trying to collect the best recipes and tabletop creations. The actual labor for the feast starts about a week out: one day for shopping, one day for setting the table, and about three days for cooking. And I do not spend those three days cooking all new recipes. Oh, no—I am a believer in combining the new with some of the tried-and-true favorites. That way if any of my culinary experiments do not work out, I am not left "empty-plated." And I welcome comments about what people do and do not like, because a lot of my experiments will become part of my rotation of recipes for the next year. Thanksgiving truly is a great time to operate as a test kitchen because you have such a captive and honest audience. (They are family, after all!) So I say welcome Thanksgiving as a time for you to bond not only with your family but also with your kitchen.

HAPPY THANKSGIVING
FRAME WREATH

This is a great way to reuse old frames. If you have a picture frame that's missing glass or backing, it's ideal for this project.

Materials

PRINTABLE IRON-ON TRANSFERS

PLAIN FABRIC, SUCH AS COTTON OR MUSLIN

LARGE EMPTY PICTURE FRAME

Tools

STAPLE GUN

SCISSORS

IRON

- On your computer, pick a large and festive font and type out your holiday message. Choose font and size according to the dimensions of your frame.

- Because you're printing on transfer paper, you'll need to select the option "flip horizontal" when you print.

- Print out the transfer and iron it onto the fabric, following the directions on the transfer package.

- Trim the fabric to size and staple it onto the back of the frame. You don't have to fill up the entire frame with fabric; you can use a smaller piece and staple it diagonally within the frame.

- Hang the frame on your door and adorn it with a seasonal garland.

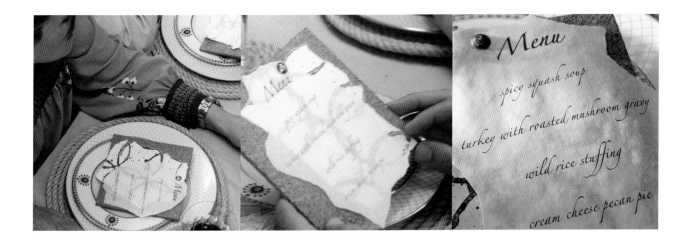

COFFEE-STAINED CORK MENUS

I don't drink coffee, but I must say I like watching the various colors that coffee forms on these menus.

Materials

COFFEE GROUNDS
WATER
WHITE OR CREAM-COLORED PAPER
TRANSLUCENT PAPER
THUMBTACKS
SMALL CORK SQUARES

Tools

DRINKING GLASS

- Mix 2 cups of coffee grounds with ½ cup of water to create a dipping paste for the paper. For each menu, dip your glass in the paste, then place it on a sheet of paper to create the pattern of your choice—we've chosen a chain-link effect that overlaps a bit.

- Let the paper dry and brush off any excess coffee grounds.

- Choose a scripted font to give the menus an elegant touch. Print out each dinner menu on the translucent paper.

- Tear the edges off the translucent paper and the coffee-stained paper. Place the translucent paper with the menu on top of the coffee-stained paper.

- Attach these to the cork squares with thumbtacks.

Menu

spicy squash soup

turkey with roasted mushroom gravy

wild rice stuffing

cream cheese pecan pie

CORK RUNNER AND NUTS IN VASES

If you don't have many nuts, or are trying to cut costs, place a block of Styrofoam or other filler (smaller than the vase) in the bottom middle of the vase—you'll see only the outside layer of nuts and use half as many!

Materials

VARIOUS SHELLED NUTS

ASSORTED LARGE CYLINDRICAL VASES

LARGE CORK SQUARES

- Fill the vases with assorted nuts.

- Place the large cork squares along your dinner table as a runner and position the vases on top of the squares.

SPICY BUTTERNUT SQUASH SOUP

Serves 12

When making soup, always pay close attention to the ratios of liquids to solids. If you learn these ratios, you'll be on your way to making up your own recipes. Also, if a soup seems too thick, add a little more stock; cooking is all about improvising, and this soup is no exception!

3	WHOLE BUTTERNUT SQUASHES
1	TEASPOON CINNAMON
½	CUP LIGHT BROWN SUGAR
1	STICK BUTTER, CUBED
1	TABLESPOON SALT, PLUS MORE TO TASTE
¼	CUP OLIVE OIL
2	ONIONS, SLICED THIN
4	GARLIC CLOVES, CRUSHED
	3-INCH PIECE GINGER, PEELED AND SLICED THIN
2	LEEKS, SLICED THIN, WHITE PART ONLY
1	SMALL CARROT, PEELED AND SLICED THIN
¾	TEASPOON CRUSHED RED PEPPER
4	CUPS CHICKEN STOCK
	3–4 CUPS WATER

1. Preheat oven to 375 degrees.

2. Peel squashes with a vegetable peeler, cut off ends, and cut in half. Remove seeds and any stringy parts from the center with a spoon and discard. Rough-cut into 1-inch squares. Place squash in a large roasting pan, sprinkle with cinnamon, brown sugar, and butter, and roast until tender, about 40 minutes, stirring often.

3. Meanwhile, heat a large soup pot on high and add olive oil. When oil is hot, add onions, garlic, leeks, carrot, and ginger. Reduce heat to medium and cook vegetables slowly, stirring often. Add pepper and stir for 1 minute.

4. Add half of the cooked squash to pot, add stock, and simmer for 20 minutes. Remove contents of pot and place in blender. (Take care, as the liquid will be hot. When pureeing hot liquids, always start the blender on a low speed, slowly increasing to a higher speed to avoid burns and messes.) Puree soup until slightly thicker than a broth.

5. Return soup to pot, add the remaining squash and the water, and simmer for an additional 20 minutes. Add salt to taste.

ROAST TURKEY

Serves 12 (makes one 16-pound turkey)

It may sound like a huge undertaking, but roasting a turkey can actually be quite simple. This salt rub is a brilliant shade of green that looks great and makes your turkey taste even better. Impress your guests and even yourself with this easy recipe!

1 16-POUND TURKEY, THAWED IF
   FROZEN

Salt Rub

½ BUNCH FRESH THYME

½ BUNCH FRESH PARSLEY

2 BAY LEAVES

3 CUPS KOSHER SALT

Turkey

½ BUNCH FRESH PARSLEY

½ BUNCH FRESH THYME

2 HEADS GARLIC, ENDS CUT OFF
   BLACK PEPPER

1. Remove neck and giblets from turkey and save for making gravy.

2. For the salt rub: in the bowl of a large food processor, combine herbs (with stems and salt). Blend well, until salt is green and herbs are finely chopped. Place turkey in a large roasting pan and generously cover entire bird, including cavity, with salt mixture.

3. Let turkey sit in refrigerator for 4 hours. After 4 hours, remove green salt, rinse turkey well with water, and pat dry completely with paper towels.

4. Preheat oven to 350 degrees.

5. While oven is heating, stuff cavity of turkey with parsley, thyme, and garlic. Season outside of bird with pepper.

6. Place turkey in a large roasting pan with a rack, and roast for 2½ hours or until the juices run clear when turkey is cut between thigh and breast.

7. Remove turkey from oven and allow it to rest for 20 minutes, covered with aluminum foil, before carving.

WILD RICE STUFFING

Serves 12 (makes one 13 x 9-inch pan)

A dark and delicious version of traditional stuffing.

3 CUPS WATER

1 TABLESPOON SALT

2 CUPS MIXED WILD RICE

1 LOAF PUMPERNICKEL BREAD, CUT INTO ¼-INCH CUBES

1 MEDIUM CARROT, PEELED (CUT INTO 4 PIECES)

1 STALK CELERY (CUT INTO 4 PIECES)

1 LARGE ONION (CUT INTO 4 PIECES)

¼ CUP OLIVE OIL

3 CUPS CHORIZO, LARGE DICE

3 CLOVES GARLIC, CHOPPED

6 SPRIGS FRESH THYME LEAVES

2 TABLESPOONS FRESH SAGE LEAVES, CHOPPED

2 TEASPOONS BLACK PEPPER, PLUS MORE TO TASTE

4 CUPS CHICKEN STOCK

SALT TO TASTE

COOKING OIL OR NONSTICK COOKING SPRAY

1. Preheat oven to 350 degrees.

2. Bring water to a boil in a medium saucepan, add salt and rice, stir, and cover. Reduce heat to low and simmer until water is absorbed, about 35 minutes. Rice will still be a bit underdone at this point, but that is okay.

3. Remove rice and place in a large mixing bowl.

4. Place cubed pumpernickel on a large sheet tray and toast in the oven until dry, about 8 minutes, then add to rice.

5. Chop all vegetables in a food processor to a small dice, pulsing to keep everything evenly cut.

6. Heat a large sauté pan on high and add olive oil. Once oil is hot, add chorizo and brown well. Add chopped vegetables, garlic, and herbs, reduce heat to medium, and cook, stirring often, until onions are soft. Add mixture to rice and bread, and combine well.

7. In a small sauce pot, bring chicken stock to a boil. Oil or spray a 13 x 9-inch pan and spread the stuffing evenly in the pan. Pour chicken stock over stuffing and bake until most of the liquid is absorbed, about 40 minutes.

MUSHROOM GRAVY

Serves 12 (makes 8 cups)

And what would a turkey be without the gravy?

4 TABLESPOONS VEGETABLE OIL

NECK AND GIBLETS FROM TURKEY

2 SMALL CARROTS, PEELED (LARGE DICE)

2 STALKS CELERY (LARGE DICE)

2 LARGE ONIONS (LARGE DICE)

3 CLOVES GARLIC, CRUSHED

4 SPRIGS FRESH THYME

1 BAY LEAF

10 CUPS CHICKEN STOCK

8 OUNCES MUSHROOMS (PRESLICED)

2 TABLESPOONS RED WINE VINEGAR

2 TABLESPOONS UNSALTED BUTTER

4 TABLESPOONS CHOPPED SHALLOTS

2 TABLESPOONS FLOUR

SALT AND BLACK PEPPER TO TASTE

1. Heat a large soup pot on high and add 2 tablespoons of the oil. Once oil is hot, add turkey neck and giblets, and brown on all sides until a dark golden color is achieved, about 5 minutes. Add carrots, celery, onions, and garlic, and continue stirring. Cook vegetables until onions are translucent and slightly colored. Add thyme, bay leaf, and chicken stock, and lower heat to a simmer.

2. Allow liquid to simmer at least 45 minutes, skimming off any grease with a ladle. Strain out solids with a fine-mesh strainer or colander, discard solids, and reserve stock.

3. Heat a large sauce pot on high and add the remaining oil. Once oil is hot, add mushrooms and cook over high heat, allowing them to brown on all sides, about 5 minutes. When mushrooms are evenly browned, add vinegar and cook for 2 minutes. Reduce heat to medium and add butter. Allow butter to melt before adding shallots and cooking them gently for 3 minutes without coloring. Stir in flour and cook for 2 minutes.

4. Add reserved stock to mushrooms little by little, stirring constantly. Bring gravy to a simmer and continue to cook for 20 minutes. Season gravy with salt and pepper to taste and serve with turkey.

LEFTOVER TURKEY-SPAGHETTI PIE

Serves 12 (makes one 13 x 9-inch pan)

This is quite simply the perfect dish after the big event, when you're not quite ready to let the taste of the holidays go. And really, at what Thanksgiving feast are you not already thinking about what to do with the leftovers?

4	QUARTS WATER
¼	CUP PLUS ½ TEASPOON SALT
1	(1-POUND) PACKAGE SPAGHETTI
3	TABLESPOONS BUTTER
1	ONION, CHOPPED
2	CLOVES GARLIC, CHOPPED
2	(8-OUNCE) CANS SLICED OLIVES
2	(8-OUNCE) JARS PIMENTOS
1½	CUPS LEFTOVER MUSHROOM GRAVY (OR 1 CAN CREAM OF MUSHROOM SOUP)
4	CUPS CRUSHED TOMATOES, WITH JUICE
2	CUPS CHICKEN STOCK
1½	(8-OUNCE) PACKAGES CREAM CHEESE
1	TEASPOON CRUSHED RED PEPPER
4	CUPS LEFTOVER TURKEY, CHOPPED
	NONSTICK COOKING SPRAY
1	CUP BREAD CRUMBS

1. Preheat oven to 350 degrees.

2. Bring water and ¼ cup of the salt to a boil and cook pasta for 1 minute less than the package recipe.

3. Heat a large sauce pot over medium heat and add butter. Once butter is hot, add onion and garlic, and sauté until onion is soft, about 5 minutes. Add olives, pimentos, gravy, tomatoes, stock, cream cheese, pepper, and the remaining ½ teaspoon of salt. Bring liquid to a simmer and cook for 15 minutes, stirring often. Make sure cream cheese melts completely, then add turkey.

4. Add pasta to sauce and mix well. Coat a 13 x 9-inch pan with nonstick spray and add mixture, spreading evenly. Cover evenly with bread crumbs.

5. Bake until bread is toasted and pie is hot throughout, about 20 minutes. Remove pie from oven and let rest 10 minutes before cutting.

WALNUT-PECAN PIE WITH CREAM CHEESE

*Serves 6–10 (makes one
10-inch deep-dish pie)*

This is a recipe I adapted years ago from a Junior League cookbook, and it has never let me down.

1 PACKAGE CREAM CHEESE,
  SOFTENED

¾ CUP BROWN SUGAR

2 TEASPOONS VANILLA

  PINCH OF SALT

4 EGGS

1 (10-INCH) DEEP-DISH PIE CRUST

1 CUP DARK CORN SYRUP

1 CUP CHOPPED PECANS

1 CUP CHOPPED WALNUTS

1. Preheat oven to 350 degrees.

2. In a mixing bowl, combine cream cheese, ¼ cup of the
   brown sugar, 1 teaspoon of the vanilla, and salt. Once
   mixture is smooth, add 1 of the eggs and mix well.

3. Spread cream cheese mixture into pie shell. Combine the
   remaining brown sugar, vanilla, and eggs with corn syrup,
   pecans, and walnuts. Pour mixture over cream cheese.
   Bake until center of pie is set, 40–50 minutes.

12

december
HOLIDAY BRUNCH

december
HOLIDAY BRUNCH

Out of all the mornings during the course of a year, Christmas morning may be the most anticipated and magical. When I was growing up, the big event of Christmas morning was opening the presents. But I also looked forward to the delicious brunch my mother would prepare every year. Christmas brunch was the time when we all sat down as a family and savored a peaceful meal after the morning's frenzy. It was the moment that reminded us of what was really at the heart of the holidays, following the more commercial portion of the celebration. As I have gotten older, my priorities have changed, and I daresay I look forward to Christmas morning brunch even more than opening presents. And because the recipes I've chosen are quick and easy, you will be able to spend more time with your family rather than cooking away in the kitchen. So celebrate what is perhaps the most enchanting morning of the year with a brunch that is sure to become a favorite family tradition.

GIFT TOPIARY

Go green! Use multiple shades of green wrapping paper to cover these "presents." If your boxes have lids, try wrapping the lids separately. Then you can store the boxes inside one another until next Christmas.

Materials

5 BOXES IN GRADUATED SIZES

ASSORTMENT OF GREEN WRAPPING PAPER

ASSORTMENT OF GREEN RIBBON

Tools

SCISSORS

TAPE

- Wrap the boxes in wrapping paper.

- Wrap the ribbon around the boxes. The larger the box, the wider the ribbon.

- Stack the boxes beginning with the largest at the bottom, then place incrementally smaller ones atop one another.

BEJEWELED NAPKIN RINGS

The bark-covered wire we used for this project is one of our favorite materials at the Katie Brown Workshop. It may look hard to find, but you can purchase it at most craft stores. It adds a real earthy feel to just about any project, especially this one!

Materials

BARK-COVERED WIRE

GOLD WIRE

GREEN JEWELS WITH HOLES

Tools

WIRE CUTTER

- For each napkin ring, coil the bark-covered wire in approximately 2–3-inch coils.

- After four coils, cut the wire and wrap the coils by twisting one end around one point of the four coils, which will attach them all together.

- Place a jewel in the middle of a 3-inch length of gold wire, then fold both ends of the wire together and twist.

- Wrap the ends of the gold wire around one of the bark-covered coils. Repeat the previous two steps on at least two different spots somewhere on the four coils.

PINECONE RUNNER

I never get tired of decorating with pinecones. To me they are one of Mother Nature's most beautiful creations.

Materials

GREEN FABRIC
STITCH WITCHERY
FLORAL WIRE
GREEN WIRE-EDGE RIBBON
FOUR PINECONES

Tools

IRON
RULER
CHALK
SCISSORS
GLUE GUN

- Measure your tabletop.

- Cut the fabric 18 inches wide and 3 feet longer than the tabletop.

- Lay the fabric facedown.

- Fold both long sides in one inch. Insert Stitch Witchery into the fold and iron the fabric to create a hem.

- Cut each end into two points. Fold the exposed edges in, insert Stitch Witchery, and iron to create a hem.

- Wrap 3–4 inches of the wire around the large end of a pinecone, leaving a few inches to come out the end. With the top few inches of the wire, poke a hole in a fabric point and fold back wire, creating a hook to attach pinecone to fabric.

- With the ribbon, tie a bow where the pinecone meets the fabric. Repeat on the other points of the runner.

PEAR SALAD WITH JICAMA, RADISH, AND CELERY

Serves 12

To keep the pears from browning after they've been cut, mix with a little lemon juice to avoid oxidation.

8-9 RADISHES, CUT IN HALF AND SLICED THIN

2 WHOLE JICAMAS, PEELED AND GRATED OR CUT INTO MATCHSTICKS

2 STALKS CELERY, PEELED AND SLICED THIN

6 BOSC PEARS, SLICED THIN

ZEST OF 3 LIMES

JUICE OF 2 LEMONS

¼ CUP OLIVE OIL

1 TABLESPOON HONEY

SALT AND BLACK PEPPER TO TASTE

Mix all ingredients in a bowl and serve. Make sure to cut the pears last, as they will oxidize.

CHOPPED GREEN SALAD

Serves 12

This salad is so rich and filling, it is a meal in itself. Enjoy!

Salad

4 CUPS CHOPPED ROMAINE

4 CUPS CHOPPED SPINACH

2 CUPS CHOPPED GREEN BELL PEPPER

2 CUPS CHOPPED CUCUMBER

2 CUPS CHOPPED ZUCCHINI

2 CUPS CHOPPED AVOCADO

¾ CUP SMALL CAPERS

SALT AND BLACK PEPPER TO TASTE

Dressing

1 CUP GRATED PARMESAN

JUICE OF 2 LEMONS

1 TABLESPOON BLACK PEPPER

1 CUP MAYONNAISE

¼ CUP EXTRA-VIRGIN OLIVE OIL

1. For the salad: in a large bowl, combine chopped greens, vegetables, and capers.

2. For the dressing: in a food processor, combine Parmesan, lemon juice, pepper, and mayonnaise. Keep the food processor running and slowly add oil in a steady stream. Reserve dressing in refrigerator until ready for use.

3. Add Parmesan dressing to salad. Toss well and season to taste with salt and pepper.

TURKEY BACON EGGS

Serves 12

What brunch would be complete without bacon and eggs? I love this dish because it combines both of them in a quick and easy fashion.

12 3-INCH RAMEKINS

   OLIVE OIL OR NONSTICK COOKING SPRAY

36 PIECES TURKEY BACON

4 TABLESPOONS OLIVE OIL OR BUTTER

4 SHALLOTS, CHOPPED FINE

2 SMALL BAGS BABY ARUGULA (OR SPINACH)

12 EGGS

2 CUPS GRATED GRUYÈRE CHEESE

   SALT AND BLACK PEPPER TO TASTE

1. Preheat oven to 350 degrees.

2. Prepare ramekins by brushing insides with olive oil or spraying with nonstick spray. Wrap 2 pieces of bacon around inside of each ramekin, closing all gaps around the sides. Cut the remaining 12 pieces of bacon in half. Place 2 of these pieces in bottom of each ramekin, covering all gaps.

3. Heat a large sauté pan on high, add olive oil or butter, add shallots, and reduce heat to medium. Gently cook shallots until translucent, about 4 minutes. Add arugula to pan and cook until wilted. Remove arugula from pan and allow to cool. Squeeze out any excess water with your hands.

4. Combine eggs, Gruyère, and arugula, season with salt and pepper. (Remember that the cheese will add some salt of its own.) Fill each ramekin three-quarters full and bake until eggs are set and tops are golden and puffed, about 20 minutes.

5. Remove bacon and eggs from ramekins while hot, using towels to prevent burning yourself. Serve immediately, as eggs will lose volume as they sit.

GINGER PANCAKE ROLL-UPS

Serves 12
(makes 12–14 pancakes)

I think my mother got this recipe from the back of a box years ago, and it has turned into a Brown family classic. I promise, if you try it, it will inevitably get into your rotation.

Pancakes

2   CUPS BISQUICK BISCUIT MIX

1   TEASPOON CINNAMON

½   TEASPOON CLOVES

½   TEASPOON GINGER

1   EGG

1½ CUPS MILK

VEGETABLE OIL FOR BRUSHING PAN

2   (8-OUNCE) PACKAGES CREAM CHEESE

Sauce

½   CUP BUTTER, MELTED

1   EGG, WELL BEATEN

1   CUP SUGAR

ZEST OF 1 LEMON

¼   CUP WATER

3   TABLESPOONS LEMON JUICE

1. For the pancakes: mix dry ingredients, then slowly add wet; mix well into a smooth batter. Heat a pancake griddle or nonstick pan on medium-high and brush with oil. Ladle batter onto griddle and cook pancakes on one side until bubbles are visible on top, then flip and cook other side until golden.

2. Cut each cream cheese package into 6 pieces. Roll each pancake around piece of cream cheese.

3. For the sauce: in a medium saucepan over medium heat, gradually add ingredients one at a time, beating well. Continue stirring constantly (otherwise egg will cook) until mixture thickens slightly.

4. To serve, pour warm sauce over pancake roll-ups.

TOMATO BREAD PUDDING

Serves 12
(makes one 13 x 9-inch pan)

This is a great way to use up tomatoes and bread that are about to go. Combine them with cheese and spices, and you will have a delicious pudding.

2   TABLESPOONS OLIVE OIL

1   LARGE ONION, DICED

4   CLOVES GARLIC, CHOPPED

5   TABLESPOONS FRESH THYME

1¼ CUPS HEAVY CREAM

2¼ CUPS CHICKEN STOCK

1   TABLESPOON SALT

1½ TEASPOONS BLACK PEPPER

2   EGGS

10 CUPS CUBED FRENCH BREAD
    (MEDIUM-SIZE CUBES)

2½ CUPS GRATED PARMESAN

6   CUPS HALVED CHERRY
    TOMATOES

1. Preheat oven to 350 degrees.

2. Heat a medium-size sauté pan over high heat and add olive oil. When oil is hot, add onion, garlic, and thyme. Lower heat to medium and cook until onion is soft, about 6 minutes. Place mixture in a large mixing bowl and allow to cool. Add cream, stock, salt, pepper, and eggs, and whisk until well combined.

3. Add bread, Parmesan, and tomatoes, tossing well to coat everything, and allow mixture to sit for at least 10 minutes. Place in a greased 13 x 9-inch pan and bake until top is golden brown and pudding is set, about 45 minutes.

LEMON GRANITA

Serves 12

This is an easy way to create an elegant dessert that will be light and refreshing.

4 CUPS SUGAR

3 CUPS WATER

3 CUPS FRESH LEMON JUICE

FRESH MINT LEAVES OR
LEMON SLICES FOR GARNISH

1. Heat sugar and water on medium heat, stirring until sugar dissolves. Add lemon juice and stir to combine.

2. Pour mixture into a 15 x 9½ x 2½-inch glass baking dish. Place in freezer and stir with a rubber spatula every 20 minutes until completely frozen, breaking up any large lumps.

3. Serve granita in glasses, garnished with fresh mint or lemon slices.

MIX-AND-MATCH MENUS

It might go without saying that I love good entertaining books. One of the things I love most about them is learning from the way the author-chefs put their menus together. Seeing what side dishes they pair with main courses and which desserts they feel match to make a whole meal. I learn from the different occasions they believe fit best with each combination. However, sometimes I feel people follow the lead of the author too closely and forget to use the book not only for entertaining but also as a great cookbook or a fantastic source for many a fine recipe. In fact, these are books you can use to invent your own recipe combinations. That is why I have created the following menu selections, I want to encourage you, the reader, to mix it up and combine any which way. Take some of the recipes from the various chapters and form them into customized menus that will fit your occasion. Come on; shake it up and get cooking!

Garden Lunch

CHOPPED GREEN SALAD **(December)**

PARMESAN SOUP WITH SWISS CHARD–STUFFED DUMPLINGS **(January)**

DEEP-DISH COUNTRY QUICHE **(May)**

GINGER PANCAKE ROLL-UPS **(December)**

CHUNKY APPLE POPOVERS WITH BROWN SUGAR MASCARPONE CREAM **(February)**

Winter Dinner

HONEY-SPICED ALMONDS **(June)**

HERBED FETA PUFFS **(March)**

PEAR SALAD WITH JICAMA, RADISH, AND CELERY **(December)**

WHITE BEAN–LAMB STEW **(February)**

MUFFIN TIN COOKIES X 2 **(July)**

Outdoor Picnic

PEPPER-BREAD SALAD WITH BALSAMIC VINAIGRETTE **(July)**

CORN FRITTERS **(July)**

GRILLED PORK RIBS **(August)**

WALNUT-PECAN PIE WITH CREAM CHEESE **(November)**

Early Sunday Dinner

GREEN GARDEN SOUP **(May)**

WILD RICE STUFFING **(November)**

GRILLED HANGER STEAK SANDWICH WITH CARAMELIZED PEARL ONIONS **(October)**

CHOCOLATE CHUNKS WITH CHERRIES AND PISTACHIOS **(January)**

CINNAMON-SUGAR CRISPS WITH ORANGE CRÈME FRAÎCHE **(February)**

Kids' Special

POPCORN GRAB BAGS (April)

SPICY CHICKEN WINGS (July)

ZEBRA MAC 'N' CHEESE (September)

APPLE BROWNIES (August)

Flavor Fare

ENDIVE SALAD WITH WATER-CRESS AND GRAPEFRUIT (January)

MOROCCAN BRAISED CHICKEN (June)

BIBB WRAPS WITH ORZO SALAD (March)

PASSION FRUIT CRÈME POTS (October)

Hearty Homemade Supper

CUCUMBER SALAD WITH MARI-NATED RED ONION AND FRESH HERBS (March)

HERBED PASTA SALAD WITH GARLIC AIOLI CREAM (October)

BEEF BRISKET (August)

LEMON GRANITA (December)

Happy Birthday

MOROCCAN CARROT SALAD (June)

CITRUS SHRIMP (July)

GRILLED SIDE OF SALMON (October)

LEMON-RHUBARB TRIFLE (May)

Everyday Dinner

HONEY AND MINT MANGO SALAD (September)

SCALLION-MINT COUSCOUS (June)

HERBED FLATBREAD (October)

MARINATED CHICKEN KEBABS WITH LEMON-PEPPER YOGURT SAUCE (March)

PEANUT BRITTLE (August)

Brunch Bunch

PERFECT CROSTINI WITH WARM BLACKBERRY CHUTNEY (February)

PARMESAN-CAYENNE SCONES (May)

LEFTOVER TURKEY–SPAGHETTI PIE (November)

TURKEY BACON EGGS (December)

SESAME-HONEY CAKES (June)

Candlelight Dinner

SPICY BUTTERNUT SQUASH SOUP (November)

MANCHEGO-ARUGULA SALAD WITH POMEGRANATE VINAIGRETTE (February)

TOMATO BREAD PUDDING (December)

FILET OF BEEF PILED HIGH WITH MUSHROOMS AND FRIED LEEKS (January)

CHOCOLATE-SPICE CAKE (March)

Back-to-School

VEGGIE STRIP MOUNTAIN (September)

WHOLE-GRAIN POTATO SALAD (August)

PIZZA STICK ROLL-UPS (April)

POKE CUPCAKES (May)

Holiday Party

PROSCIUTTO AND ASPARAGUS MELTS (March)

STACKED SALAD WITH AVOCADO DRESSING (May)

ROAST TURKEY (November)

GORGONZOLA-STUFFED POTATOES (January)

WAFER CAKE (April)

Picture Index

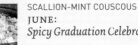

Salads

Sauces

Desserts

EASY CHOCOLATE MOUSSE, THREE WAYS   25
JANUARY:
A New Year's Evening

CHOCOLATE CHUNKS WITH CHERRIES AND PISTACHIOS   27
JANUARY:
A New Year's Evening

CINNAMON-SUGAR CRISPS WITH ORANGE CRÈME FRAÎCHE   41
FEBRUARY:
A Birthday Valentine

CHUNKY APPLE POPOVERS WITH BROWN SUGAR–MASCARPONE CREAM   43
FEBRUARY:
A Birthday Valentine

CHOCOLATE-SPICE CAKE   59
MARCH:
The Welcome Wagon

LEMON-RHUBARB TRIFLE   87
MAY:
Feminine Fete

POKE CUPCAKES   87
MAY:
Feminine Fete

POPCORN GRAB BAGS   67
APRIL:
Kids' Day

BROWNIE PUDDING POPS   71
APRIL:
Kids' Day

WAFER CAKE   73
APRIL:
Kids' Day

SESAME-HONEY CAKES   103
JUNE:
Spicy Graduation Celebration

MUFFIN TIN COOKIES X 2   117
JULY:
Beach Picnic

PEANUT BRITTLE   130
AUGUST:
Family Cookout

APPLE BROWNIES   131
AUGUST:
Family Cookout

ELEPHANT TRUNKS   144
SEPTEMBER:
Playful Safari Spread

INSECT JIGGLERS   145
SEPTEMBER:
Playful Safari Spread

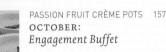
PASSION FRUIT CRÈME POTS   157
OCTOBER:
Engagement Buffet

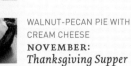
WALNUT-PECAN PIE WITH CREAM CHEESE   171
NOVEMBER:
Thanksgiving Supper

LEMON GRANITA   183
DECEMBER:
Holiday Brunch

Centerpieces

ALL THAT GLITTERS   15
JANUARY:
A New Year's Evening

DESSERT REFLECTION TRAY   16
JANUARY:
A New Year's Evening

PARTY BALLS   17
JANUARY:
A New Year's Evening

NOT-SO-EMPTY NEST   33
FEBRUARY:
A Birthday Valentine

PRETTY LITTLE PICTURE   79
MAY:
Feminine Fete

SPARKLING STICKS   95
JUNE:
Spicy Graduation Celebration

FRUIT OR VEGGIE CENTERPIECES   122
AUGUST:
Family Cookout

Acknowledgments

Some people say working for me can only be gauged in dog years. In some ways, I am sorry to say I agree with them. But I also believe that the time, energy, and dedication of all the talented people who gathered to create this book are immeasurable. These pages come to life because of them: their spirit and their teamwork. And I thank them from the bottom of my heart.

Stephanie DiTullio. It was such fun to sit back and watch you do your styling thing. I believe it takes an immense amount of talent and history to get me to sit back and watch. Thank you; it was such a pleasure.

Jess Ryan. I know that you know that I know and we all know that you are the bomb and perhaps the most gifted person I have had the pleasure to work with. Do not ever stop.

Kaegan Welch. You taught me a ton, and it was my great honor to have you in our kitchens. Your perfectionism was a lesson to me. And I am forever grateful that you took time out of your travels to lend us your talents for this book.

Holly Moore. You have a combination of blessings that are going to take you right where you want to go. Thank you for making a stop on your way up to be with us in the development and creation of this book. And I will be forever grateful for your mac 'n' cheese!

Kyle Stewart. Do not even think of ever leaving me because you are simply *real* good. Your monkeys, your mailbox, and your humor are all over this book. I knew from the moment you came to interview that you would at least make us laugh. Little did I know that you were a secret crafter, a customer service department, a Filofax, an accountant, a human-resources expert, and a talent coordinator all in one. My gratitude runs deep.

Erin Selmer. Even though you came late to the party, you have become the life of it. Your written words and eye for style inform our shops, and I am in debt to your determination to get it right. I look forward to what I hope will be a fruitful collaboration for us both.

Paul Whicheloe. You have been my longest collaborator—I believe we are going on ten years. I have gained so much from your eyes and your ability. Never go away, okay? No matter how late, how long, or how many pictures we have to take in a day. Okay?

Evan/Esther/Eleanor McGann. You truly are one of my favorites and your patience with my Polaroid obsession is magnificent. Thank you.

Gary Tooth. I do not know how you do it every time.

Tracy Behar. Thank you for your calm delivery and constant coaxing.

Ira Silverberg. You really do always have my best interests at heart, and I look forward to many a moon with you and yours.

To all the bright faces that shine on these pages: Jackie Lowey and Rebecca and Jonathan Kuperschmid; India Galesi Grant and Christina Galesi; Lisa, David, Adelia, and Everett Rattray; Evelyn and Ava Delorenzo; Charlotte and Evan Johnson and Laurie Gordon; Adeline, Gillian, Amelie, and Nicki Neubert; Malachy Mitchnick and Vivienne Keegan; Egan Barzilay; and of course, Benjamin and Charley DiTullio. Thank you for showing up and partying with us.

To Zara Ingilizian, Sara Braun, Cynthia Liu, Liz Carboni, and Louis Roloff. Thanks for being truly great and gracious corporate partners.

To Dennis Thomas, Tommy Paulk, and everyone else at Bonnie Plants. Who knew I would find such great supports in Union Springs?

Pam and Lynch's Garden Center. The world will never know how empty our pages would look without your generous contribution and knowledge.

To Chuck Adams and everyone else at the Companion Group. You really are our West Coast tribesman. I am so happy to call you the better half.

Mom, Dad, Lynn, Marlee, Bing, Dan, Bob, Meredith, Paul, Charlie, Jack, Mimi, Tilly, Quattro, Maverick, Patsy, Jimmy, Dick, Gail, Bridgit, Bud, Sandra, Corey, Isaac, Corbin, John, and Lillian. Your love is all over these pages.

To Nancy Banks, Sarah Essex, Tori Horowitz, Mariska Hargitay, and Martha McCully. Never give up on the thought that someday I will be a lady who has time to lunch.

To my husband. How I got so lucky, I will never know.